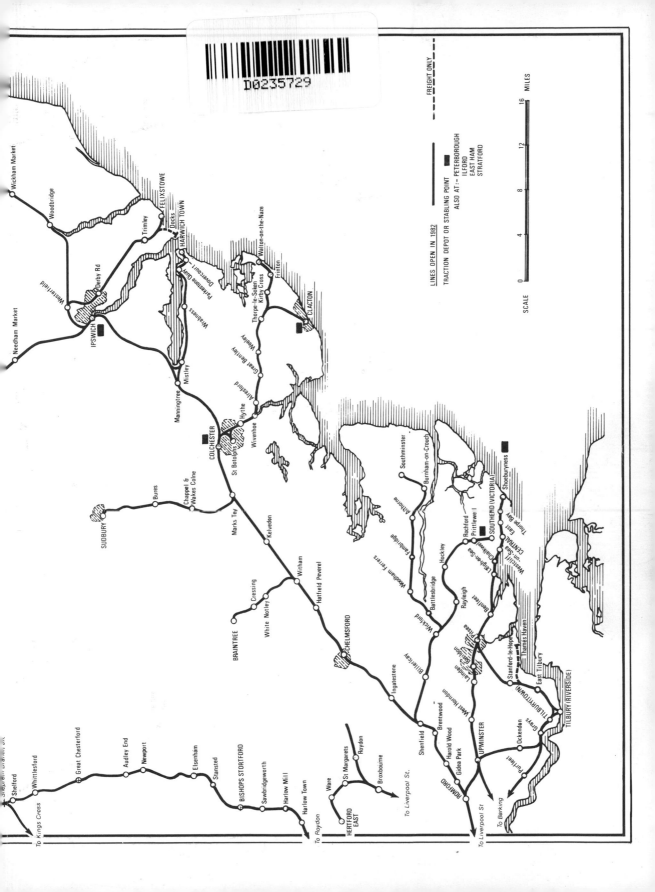

LINES OPEN IN 1982
TRACTION DEPOT OR STABLING POINT ■
ALSO AT :– PETERBOROUGH
ILFORD
EAST HAM
STRATFORD

FREIGHT ONLY

SCALE

0   4   8   12   16
MILES

Wickham Market
Woodbridge
Westerfield
Needham Market
IPSWICH
Derby Rd
Trimley
FELIXSTOWE
Docks
HARWICH TOWN
Dovercourt
Parkeston Quay
Walton-on-the-Naze
Frinton
Kirby Cross
Thorpe-le-Soken
Weeley
Great Bentley
CLACTON
Mistley
Manningtree
Alresford
Wrabness
Hythe
Wivenhoe
COLCHESTER
St Botolphs
Bures
Chappel & Wakes Colne
SUDBURY
Marks Tey
Kelvedon
Witham
Hatfield Peverel
Cressing
White Notley
BRAINTREE
Southminster
Burnham-on-Crouch
Althorne
Woodham Ferrers
Fambridge
Hockley
Battlesbridge
Wickford
CHELMSFORD
Ingatestone
Billericay
Rayleigh
Prittlewell
Rochford
SOUTHEND (VICTORIA)
Shoeburyness
Thorpe Bay
SOUTHEND CENTRAL
Westcliff-on-Sea
Chalkwell
Leigh-on-Sea
Benfleet
Pitsea
Laindon
Basildon
Stanford-le-Hope
East Tilbury
Thames Haven
TILBURY (RIVERSIDE)
TILBURYTOWN
Grays
Ockendon
Purfleet
UPMINSTER
ROMFORD
Gidea Park
Harold Wood
West Horndon
Brentwood
Shenfield
To Liverpool St
To Barking
To Liverpool St
Sheprell Branch Jn.
Shelford
Whittlesford
Great Chesterford
Audley End
Newport
Elsenham
Stansted
BISHOPS STORTFORD
Sawbridgeworth
Harlow Mill
Harlow Town
Roydon
St Margarets
Ware
HERTFORD EAST
Broxbourne
To Roydon
To Kings Cross
To Liverpool St.

East Anglian
RAILS IN THE 1980s

Michael J. Collins

LONDON

IAN ALLAN LTD

To my wife Margaret,
for her help and understanding.

On a freezing 10 December 1981 Class 47 No 47.002 approaches Cattishall Crossing, east of Bury St Edmunds with the 20.07 Coatbridge-Felixstowe. *John C. Baker*

First published 1983

ISBN 0 7110 1310 1

Published by Ian Allan Ltd, Shepperton, Surrey; and printed by Ian Allan Printing Ltd at their works at Coombelands in Runnymede, England

Contents

Preface   **7**

**Inter-City on the Norwich/
Yarmouth-London main line**   **8**

**Inter-City to Cambridge and
Kings Lynn**   **22**

**Maritime Services: Freight to
the East Anglian Ports**   **36**

General Freight Services   **48**

**Cross-Country Passenger
Services**   **64**

Branch Lines   **77**

**Locomotive, Unit and Rolling
Stock Maintenance**   **88**

Commuter Services   **95**

Passenger Specials   **101**

Behind the Scenes   **106**

Photographed running over two hours late because of a locomotive failure on the East Suffolk line is the 07.22 Lowestoft-Liverpool Street passing south of Bentley station (closed November 1960) with Class 31 No 31.402 supplying traction on 5 April 1982. *Michael J. Collins*

Preface

Line closures in the past have brought the BR network in East Anglia to the point where any further reduction in services or line closures could well have a knock-on effect and plunge the whole system into serious decline. The operating authorities have been aware of this and in these terms the late 1970s and early 1980s have been an era of stability for railways in East Anglia with only subtle changes of service provision taking place.

At the time of writing in 1982 major changes are on the horizon which will affect the pace of change on the East Anglian railway network. Further electrification is in the advanced planning stage, finance has been promised though is not yet forthcoming, major resignalling work based on the ambitious Colchester and Cambridge schemes is already taking place, and redevelopment of stations are either in the discussion stage or pipeline. The old world charm of manual crossings, semaphore signalling, and labour intensive operating is fast disappearing. The harsh economic climate in the 1980s and changes in the Road Transport Acts are having their effects, and many branch lines look threatened as a consequence. The ageing DMU fleet staggers on reluctantly, 20-year old diesel locomotives, fast approaching life expiry, still see passenger service. Great changes can not be far away.

The aim of this book has been to focus on the East Anglian rail services — passenger and freight — at the beginning of the 1980s, and to endeavour to depict present operations in words and photographs. In doing so I have tried to be mindful of the historical setting and have tried to consider the effect which future innovations may have.

A major difficulty encountered in the preparation of this book has been in trying to pin down a definition of exactly which area constitutes 'East Anglia'. No two academics or scholars seem to have the same view, an East Anglian division does not exist in BR operating parlance, and the area does not appear to have an accepted geographical definition.

For these reasons a very liberal view of the extent of the area has been selected; all remaining lines belonging to the former Great Eastern Railway have been encompassed, and the Great Northern/Great Eastern Joint Line as far as Spalding has been considered as being within the region. For the sake of completeness, a glimpse of the workings on the London, Tilbury & Southend network out of Fenchurch Street has been included.

The book is essentially a look at the rich variety of services traversing the East Anglian lines and a great many of these trains either emanate from or are focused on travel to London. In addition a large proportion of the locomotives and units at work within the region look to the facilities of depots within the metropolis for servicing and maintenance facilities. Therefore some lines within the London area have had to be included despite not being within the East Anglia area in the strictest sense.

In the preparation of the work I have travelled many thousands of miles both by rail and road. In all of these miles I have encountered nothing but interest and friendliness from the many railway staff, members of the travelling public, railway enthusiasts, or fellow photographers that have been met. Some of these people have become firm friends and have assisted with information or photographs from their own collections. I thank them all but in particular I wish to specially thank Mr Kim Fullbrook, former president of the Cambridge University Railway Club for his assistance in reading the text. A special mention must go to Mr Michael Oakley of the Diesel & Electric Group for his help and advice and also to my friend Colin Marsden who, with great tact, critically appraised the photographic content of the book.

I hope that readers enjoy browsing through this volume as much as I have enjoyed preparing it.

Michael J. Collins
Colchester
September 1982

Inter-City on the Norwich/ Yarmouth-London main line

Probably the premier service from London (Liverpool Street) station is the hourly service of trains to Norwich, with the fastest services taking just under two hours for the journey. It is ironic, however, that despite the fast Inter-City image portrayed by BR, some timings still compare unfavourably with those achieved with steam before the war.

At the beginning of the 1980s the Norwich line services were operated by rakes of Mark 2a steam heated carriage stock. The transition to Mark 2d/2f air-conditioned stock was delayed for some time but in December 1980 the Western Region was able to release a number of sets of these carriages made redundant by increasing use of High Speed Trains. At the time of writing all but one early morning and late evening service use the newly acquired stock.

In the past, much of the rolling stock providing the Norwich services had to be stabled overnight in the open at Great Yarmouth. This necessitated up early morning services starting from Yarmouth and many of the evening down services being extended,

in order to terminate there. This practice dated from 1962 when Yarmouth lost its through service to London via the East Suffolk Line, but ceased during October 1982, because the open accommodation was not really suitable for sophisticated modern vehicles. The completion of the £7 million Crown Point Depot at Norwich enabled the problem to be resolved because the depot had facilities for the stabling and maintenance of carriage stock built in. This enabled a reduction in the number of Liverpool Street-Norwich services which had to work through to, or start from, Yarmouth purely for operating convenience.

All Norwich/Yarmouth to Liverpool Street services are now routed via the GE Colchester main line except one up and one down summer dated service which runs via Cambridge and an early morning

Under the Wires

Below: Liverpool Street is the gateway to East Anglia and in this view No 47.568 backs on to the 09.30 train to Norwich on a very chilly 16 January 1982. *Michael J. Collins*

Norwich-Liverpool Street train which also takes this route. In the 1981/82 passenger timetable some late evening trains also took this route but they were withdrawn on the grounds of economy. Late evening passengers now have to travel to King's Cross by way of a local Cambridge train and then changing to a Royston service, where the electrified line to the capital is reached.

The basic pattern of Norwich line services is arranged so that alternate trains stop at the intermediate stations of Manningtree (for connection to Harwich Town), Stowmarket and Diss; while on Saturdays some trains stop additionally at Chelmsford. The fast trains stop at Colchester and Ipswich only. One up morning service and one down evening service omits the Colchester stop altogether and runs fast to and from Ipswich. These two trains have been dubbed 'The East Anglian' by railway staff and are the only trains to run in the UK with a headboard regularly attached to the front of the locomotive.

Much of the GE main line is now passed for 95mph running by passenger trains with 100mph passed between Colchester and Chelmsford in mid-1982. There is a 60mph speed limit through the curve at Chelmsford station, however, and an 85mph limit at Stowmarket. Following an 80mph speed limit between Diss and Burston the final four miles to Norwich — particularly over Trowse Lower Junction — are seriously restricted.

The principal impediment for further acceleration of the Norwich services is the initial $24\frac{3}{4}$ miles from Liverpool Street to Chelmsford. After the tortuous exit from the London terminus is the 1 in 70 climb to Bethnal Green and a line limit is imposed as far as Stratford. The problem is compounded because further speed restrictions at Ilford, Gidea Park and Shenfield further impede progress. Signal sighting distances as far as Shenfield are also critical because at present they do not allow any acceleration of running to take place.

Sharing tracks with the Norwich services as far as Colchester are the hourly fast trains to Clacton. These services diverge from the Norwich main line on the down side of Colchester North station. Clacton services use a 1,200yd 'dive-under' constructed during the late 1950s in connection with a modernisation scheme for the area. The Liverpool Street-Clacton services are still handled by the over 20-year old Class 309 EMUs except on certain rush hour trains. These units, despite their age, still have impressive characteristics of acceleration and are the most reliable electric units on BR. Most of the Clacton services make stops at Chelmsford and Witham, with some rush hour and Saturday morning trains calling additionally at the village stations between Colchester and Shenfield. At the beginning of the 1980s these services boasted a buffet car on many trains but they were withdrawn in 1981 in the face of decreasing patronage.

The Harwich (Parkeston Quay) boat trains diverge from the GE main line at Manningtree South Junction for the remaining part of the journey down the Harwich Branch. The majority of such services run non-stop from the capital. The basic pattern comprises three up services and three down services daily, known as 'The Hook Continental', 'The Scandinavian' and 'The Day Continental'. At peak times these trains are supplemented by dated trains or extras. Some of the private ship operators with sea routes terminating at Harwich eg Prins Ferries have their own through rail service booked to connect with sailings. The majority of Harwich services have benefited from the receipt of Mark 2 stock cascaded from the Norwich services when the air-conditioned fleet was introduced and more recently air-conditioned stock has appeared on some boat trains.

The only additional regular Inter-City trains to use the Norwich main line joins the route at Ipswich from the East Suffolk line. This is the daily morning up and evening down through service to and from Lowestoft. The service allows a day's business in the capital for travellers with appointments after the 10.12 arrival time of the up train. The 16.50

departure time of the down service is most convenient for such travellers, allowing a useful amount of time in London. During the summer the service is augmented by an up and down dated service leaving Lowestoft and Liverpool Street in the mid-morning in order to cater for business arising from holiday traffic.

Use of the Norwich line services by the travelling public up to spring 1980 was reported to be sufficient to give BR a reasonable return. Since then it has been affected by the system-wide decline in passenger receipts due to the recession. It has not, however, been as badly affected as services in other regions such as the Western Region's high speed train services. In August 1981 the 08.00 train from Norwich was departing from Ipswich roughly two-thirds full — about 320 passengers. Taking into account the high car ownership appertaining in the area this has been regarded as a good performance.

The Eastern Region has identified only about 30 regular commuters to London from Norwich. There is another sizeable contingent from Ipswich but the amount of irregular fare payers travelling to London on business is said to be high. During 1982 a special

Below: Built in 1962 Class 309 units have been stalwarts of the Liverpool Street-Clacton services for 20 years. With the flyover on the right, an eight-car set headed by unit No 309 626 approaches Ilford on 3 July 1982 with the 11.50 service from Liverpool Street. *Michael J. Collins*

package was advertised aimed at recovering some of the first class traffic from Norwich and Ipswich lost through the effects of the recession. The package was aimed at the expense account market and included First Class (return) rail travel to London, reserved seats, a full English breakfast on the outward journey and guaranteed car parking space with parking fees for the first 24 hours included.

For the remainder of the 1980s the future of the Norwich main line looks bright. After months of doubt, rumour and counter rumour, it was announced in December 1981 that the long awaited £35 million East Anglian electrification scheme would proceed. It was reported that BR expected the Colchester/Harwich section to be electrified by 1985/86 with the Ipswich/Norwich section following on by 1987/88. Considerable accelerations will be possible after the switch on.

In addition, during summer 1981 BR announced that they intended to proceed with plans to redevelop Liverpool Street at an estimated cost of £250 million over a 10-year period. The full development was expected to include 1.2 million square feet of offices, 30,000sq ft of shops and a restructured track layout between Liverpool Street and Bethnal Green. A brighter more modern Liverpool Street, coupled with faster schedules, can only encourage Inter-City patronage on the East Anglian main lines.

Below: Dual braked Class 31 No 31.218 nears the end of its journey as it threads Manor Park station, East London, with the 10.30 (Saturdays Only, Summer Dated) Lowestoft-Liverpool Street service on 3 July 1982. This is one of the few through trains between the two centres which have survived into the 1980s. *Michael J. Collins*

Bottom: Diverting to the slow lines as it approaches Shenfield is No 47.085 *Mammoth* with a rake of Mark 2A coaches forming the 09.00 Yarmouth-Liverpool Street on 30 July 1980. The commuter lines to Southend can be seen diverging to the right of the photograph. *Michael J. Collins*

Right: Making a fast approach to Romford station is Class 47 No 47.579 *James Nightall GC* hauling the 10.30 Liverpool Street-Norwich on 3 July 1982. *Michael J. Collins*

Below: Colchester is the present limit of 25kV AC overhead electrification on the ex-GE main line although finance will be available to electrify onwards to Ipswich and Norwich during the late 1980s. Making a powerful picture is Class 47 No 47.566 as it heads the Sunday 09.20 Liverpool Street-Norwich past the last of the overhead catenary on 7 March 1982. *Michael J. Collins*

Constable Country

Left: On its way to Norwich the ex-GE main line skirts the countryside associated with the painter John Constable. In this area is one of the few remaining manual signalled stretches of the line south of Ipswich, due to be replaced on completion of the Colchester resignalling. Class 47 No 47.085 *Mammoth* powers a Norwich-London express past a rather battered and leaning concrete post signal south of Ardleigh during summer 1980. *Michael J. Collins*

Top: Electrically heated, air-conditioned rolling stock infiltrated on to Norwich line services from December 1980 after becoming redundant on the Western Region due to HST operation. Class 47 No 47.566 looks smart as it heads the 09.30 Liverpool Street-Norwich past Ardleigh on 22 June 1981. *Michael J. Collins*

Above: Recovering from a permanent way restriction is Class 47 No 47.568, photographed on 14 April 1982 as it crosses from Suffolk into Essex by way of the viaduct carrying the main line over the River Stour north of Manningtree. The train is the 12.35 Norwich-Liverpool Street loaded to the now customary nine coaches plus a buffet car. *Michael J. Collins*

Type 2 and 3 Power

Top: Since the introduction of eth stock on the Norwich line, substitutions by locomotives other than Class 47/4s have become very rare. Entering the 1,981ft long platforms of Colchester North is Class 37 No 37.110 hauling an afternoon Norwich–London service on a warm 27 August 1981.
Michael J. Collins

Above: More usual power on this Liverpool Street–Harwich (Parkeston Quay) train, timed to connect with a 'Prins Ferries' sailing, is Class 37 No 37.049 photographed charging out of London between Goodmayes and Chadwell Heath on 31 October 1981. *Michael J. Collins*

Above: Some London expresses start from Yarmouth because of stock stabling constraints and are frequently Type 2 hauled for the first leg to Norwich. The 09.00 Yarmouth-Liverpool Street is photographed approaching Wensum Junction on 15 April 1982 behind 31.403. Note the carriage washing plant on the right installed as part of the new facilities at Crown Point, Norwich, which will cut down such workings in the future. *Michael J. Collins*

Below: Certain of the Norwich-London trains were still running with the older steam heated stock during 1982. Class 31 No 31.236 was recorded preparing to leave Norwich (Thorpe) with the 18.44 train to London on the evening of 6 February 1982. *Michael J. Collins*

Left: Additional trains run between London and Yarmouth on summer Saturdays. Class 31 No 31.268 was photographed passing the remains of disused semaphore signals near Whittlingham Junction with the 08.52 (Saturdays Only, Summer Dated) Liverpool Street-Yarmouth on 26 June 1982. *Michael J. Collins*

Below: The 09.35 (Saturdays Only, Summer Dated) Yarmouth-London train is one of the few such services which run via Cambridge. On 5 June 1982 Class 31/4 No 31.405 approaches Thetford with the first up train running by this route of the summer season. *Michael J. Collins*

Bentley
and Belstead

Above: The harsh gradient of Belstead Bank gives a strenuous start to up trains restarting from the Ipswich pause, but a Class 47 usually clears the top at 60mph. Breasting the summit on 11 May 1980 is Class 47 No 47.162 heading the 07.40 Yarmouth–Liverpool Street *Michael J. Collins*

Left: The 1980/81 timetable saw the introduction of an accelerated 07.18 Yarmouth–Liverpool Street train which omitted the Colchester stop. From the outset the train ran with an 'East Anglian' headboard and, together with its corresponding afternoon down working, remains the only train on BR to run regularly thus adorned. Here, Class 47 No 47.170 *County of Norfolk* (now No 47.582), running in 'Stratford special' livery, gains Belstead summit and prepares to descend Bentley Bank with the up train of 1 October 1980. *Michael J. Collins*

Below left: Having surmounted Bentley Bank the driver eases off the power handle as Class 47 No 47.572 prepares to descend Belstead Bank in charge of the 10.30 Liverpool Street–Norwich on 20 July 1982. *Michael J. Collins*

Suffolk Glimpses

Left: Class 47 No 47.581 *Great Eastern* will be using all of the available 2,580 brake horsepower as it ascends the Gipping Valley near Stowmarket on 19 July 1982 with the 10.30 Liverpool Street-Norwich. *Michael J. Collins*

Centre left: Leaving Stowmarket and approaching Haughley Junction is Class 47 No 47.582 *County of Norfolk* threading the Suffolk countryside on 22 February 1982 in charge of the 08.30 Liverpool Street-Norwich.
Michael J. Collins

Below: At Haughley Junction, the line for Bury St Edmunds diverges from the GE main line. Passing some elderly crossing gates at the site of the long closed Haughley station is Class 47 No 47.584 *County of Suffolk* with the 11.42 Norwich-Liverpool Street, reduced to just six vehicles because of the non-availability of stock.
Michael J. Collins

Left: On weekdays the 18.44 Norwich–Liverpool Street conveys mail to the capital and was photographed passing Mellis behind Class 47 No 47.579 (later named *James Nightall GC*) on 12 July 1981. The TPO, in which mail is sorted in transit, can be seen clearly as the second vehicle behind the engine. *Chris Burton*

Below: Passing Stowmarket box on 20 August 1982 is Class 47 No 47.584 *County of Suffolk* in charge of the 10.34 Norwich–Liverpool Street. The manual signalling is still a pleasant feature of this stretch of the GE main line but will be replaced by MAS when Colchester Power Box is completed.
Michael J. Collins

Norfolk Views

Right: Many people regard East Anglian terrain as rather flat but the telephoto lens accentuates the undulating nature of the countryside in this photograph of Class 47 No 47.005 bursting out of Dunston Bridge, three miles south of Norwich, with the 14.29 to Liverpool Street in July 1980. *Chris Burton*

Below : The Norwich line expresses have become associated during the 1980s with Stratford Class 47s usually sporting a distinctive white painted roof. Occasional substitutes do occur, however, and the author was on hand to record No 47.473 of Gateshead powering past Trowse Yard box with the 11.42 to Liverpool Street on 23 February 1982. Note the Mk 1 Buffet Car still soldiering on (fourth vehicle from the engine) amid this rake of air-conditioned stock. *Michael J. Collins*

Above: In 'Stratford special' livery Class 47 No 47.583 *County of Hertfordshire* approaches the closed station at Trowse during February 1982. The locomotive received this livery during July 1981 in recognition of the wedding of HRH Prince of Wales and Lady Diana Spencer. It ran for some weeks with red, white and blue stripes within the enlarged BR logo and white stripes extended along the whole bodyside. *Michael J. Collins*

Below: With a mixture of Mk 1 and Mk 2 stock, dual heated Class 47 No 47.544 will be able to operate the steam heating equipment as it leaves Yarmouth Vauxhall with the 16.12 to Liverpool Street. *Brian Morrison*

Inter-City to Cambridge and Kings Lynn

The Cambridge/King's Lynn main line diverges from the ex-GE Norwich main line at Bethnal Green and is electrified 25kV AC as far as Bishop's Stortford. One of the delights of the line beyond this point is the elderly semaphore signalling and manual crossing gates which still existed at the time of writing. Finalised during 1980, however, a £7 million contract was signed between BR and GEC — General Signal Ltd for resignalling 56 route miles in East Anglia. Part of this contract incorporated the new Cambridge Power Box covering lines to Bishop's Stortford, Royston, Fulbourne and a point just south of Ely. Completion of the scheme will spell the end of the old world charm of this route; 14 manual signalboxes will be replaced and six level crossings will be supervised from Cambridge. Work in the immediate Cambridge area was scheduled for completion during 1982. This follows on from the remodelling of the carriage sidings and goods yard entrance which was completed in 1981 together with new carriage servicing platforms. The work made unnecessary the stabling of coaching stock adjacent to the station.

Weekday Inter-City trains on the Kings Lynn main line form a basic hourly pattern of fast or semi-fast trains to Cambridge, with every two hours a fast train being extended to Ely and all stations to King's Lynn. In the early morning and early evening, a rather anachronistic up and down Ipswich-Liverpool Street train runs which travels via Bury St Edmunds and the Chippenham Junction-Cambridge line, travelling $114\frac{1}{4}$ miles between the two centres instead of the direct $68\frac{3}{4}$.

From the beginning of January 1981 a number of services, on all regions, were axed in the cause of economy. One of the lines to suffer was the Liverpool Street-Cambridge route where, mainly on Saturdays, over a dozen through stopping trains

were discontinued. They were replaced by trains operating between Bishop's Stortford and Cambridge only, mainly using two-car diesel multiple-units. Passengers wishing to travel to and from London using these services are forced to use the electric services south of Bishop's Stortford.

The fastest through trains still take over an hour to complete the $55\frac{3}{4}$ miles from Liverpool Street to Cambridge. Acceleration of services is hampered by the crowded commuter routes south of Bishop's Stortford. Although 80mph running is permitted on the Lea Valley section, there are severe speed restrictions at Bethnal Green, Hackney Downs and Clapton Junction in the first five miles out of Liverpool Street. Progress is further impeded by the track curvature onwards to Cambridge, necessitating a 70mph maximum speed, despite the fact that the only gradient of note is the last mile of 1 in 127/107 from Stansted to Elsenham. The line speed of 70mph is maintained from Cambridge to Waterbeach, where a 60mph maximum over the fens thence to King's Lynn prevents high speed running.

In contrast to the 64 miles between Colchester and Norwich, only 25 miles of additional catenary is required on the Cambridge line to complete the extension from Bishop's Stortford. BR have for a long time stated their intention to electrify this section when funds are made available, and another possibility is the electrification of the Cambridge/Shepreth Branch Junction/Royston section to make a link with the King's Cross suburban electrification.

By late autumn 1981, the Liverpool Street-Kings Lynn route found itself with severely declining passenger receipts. Competition with the M11 motorway was blamed because the line has little to offer passengers to offset the superiority of a fast motorway link, allowing car drivers to reach London in quick time. Electrification and considerable acceleration seems to be the obvious answer in an attempt to win back traffic in the late 1980s. Another possibility is that in connection with the proposed expansion of Stansted Airport it has been suggested that 45% of the air passengers could potentially arrive by rail. This potential was considered to be more likely to become realised, if a four mile link line was built from the main line just north of Stansted Station, to a new station beside the modern terminal building. This would bring much needed new money to the line, but in any event, vigorous marketing and early electrification seems vital if this East Anglian main line is to be made viable beyond the 1980s.

London Suburban

Right: Photographed on the tightly curved approach to Hackney Downs station is Class 47 No 47.004 heading the 09.52 Cambridge-Liverpool Street service on a cold 16 January 1982. *Michael J. Collins*

Below: With the Southbury Loop diverging to the right Class 47 No 47.010 roars through Cheshunt Junction with the 14.35 Liverpool Street-Kings Lynn on 3 April 1982. *Michael J. Collins*

Above: With a surge of power Class 31 No 31.175 (with number in the front indicator box) hurtles the 12.35 Liverpool Street–Cambridge service through Broxbourne on 29 January 1982. *Michael J. Collins*

Below: Harlow has had its expanding 'new town' image acknowledged during the 1980s by stopping some Cambridge trains at Harlow Town. Class 37 No 37.089 slows for the halt with the 11.05 Liverpool Street–Cambridge on a dull 29 January 1982. *Michael J. Collins*

Above: Passing first generation searchlight signals as it enters Bishop's Stortford station is Class 37 No 37.099 hauling the 09.32 Kings Lynn-Liverpool Street train on 17 April 1980.
Michael J. Collins

Stansted

Above left: Photographed passing some attractive countryside south of Stansted is Class 31 No 31.110 (fitted with indicator discs) heading the 08.35 Liverpool Street-Kings Lynn on 13 April 1982. *Michael J. Collins*

Below left: Also on 13 April 1982 the 07.37 Liverpool Street-Cambridge, formed of elderly Mark 1 stock, was recorded between Bishop's Stortford and Stansted being hauled by Class 47 No 47.017. More Cambridge line services will be entrusted to these versatile machines as they become available from other duties.
Michael J. Collins

Left: Accelerating away from the stop at Stansted station is Class 37 No 37.099 in charge of a Cambridge–Liverpool Street semi-fast working. A feasibility study has recommended the construction of a spur from near this point to the adjacent airport if expansion plans proceed in the late 1980s. *Michael J. Collins*

Below: The 09.36 Liverpool Street–Kings Lynn is hustled north of Stansted during May 1980 with Class 31 No 31.239 at the head. The quaint 'whistle' board adds character to the scene. *Michael J. Collins*

WHISTLE

Above: The 09.35 Liverpool Street-Cambridge approaches Stansted station on 13 April 1982 with Class 31 No 31.160 in charge. *Michael J. Collins*

Essex Border

Left: The GE Cambridge main line runs parallel to the Essex border with Hertfordshire for several miles north of Bishop's Stortford. Passing a delightful semaphore signal at Elsenham is Class 37 No 37.039 hauling the 14.39 Cambridge-Liverpool Street on 10 May 1980. *Michael J. Collins*

Below left: Approaching the end of a temporary speed restriction at Newport, Essex, is ex-works Class 37 No 37.116 hauling the 10.32 Cambridge-Liverpool Street on 3 August 1981.
Michael J. Collins

Right: Forging towards London through the heavily wooded Audley End cutting is Class 31 No 31.110 hauling a Cambridge-Liverpool Street working during April 1982. The south portal of Audley End tunnel can be discerned near the horizon. *Michael J. Collins*

Below: Emerging from Littlebury Tunnel whilst braking for a temporary speed restriction is Class 31 No 31.173 hauling the 14.05 Liverpool Street-Cambridge on 13 April 1982. The signals on the left will be replaced in 1983 as part of the Cambridge resignalling scheme. *Michael J. Collins*

Above: This seven coach train is no match for Class 37 No 37.115 as it scuttles towards Littlebury during spring 1982 with an early afternoon Cambridge–Liverpool Street working. *Michael J. Collins*

Below: Passing fine examples of semaphore signalling at Great Chesterford is Class 31 No 31.173 hauling the 16.10 Cambridge–Liverpool Street. It is sad to think that this beautiful structure will shortly be considered life expired and replaced by MAS. *Michael J. Collins*

Right: This elderly building is the crossing keeper's hut at Great Chesterford and is due for a shaking as Class 47 No 47.005 accelerates away from the station with the 16.05 Liverpool Street-Cambridge during Spring 1982.
Michael J. Collins

Cambridge Roundabout

Below: Catching a shaft of sunlight on a very dull day during November 1981 is Class 37 No 37.090 hauling an up Saturday morning Cambridge-Liverpool Street service past Whittlesford.
Michael J. Collins

Above: Shepreth Branch Junction box will be replaced when the new Cambridge power box is 'switched in' but it adds interest to the picture of Class 37 No 37.054 passing with the 10.32 Cambridge-Liverpool Street on 28 July 1981. *Colin J. Marsden*

Left: With the former branch to Fordham Junction diverging to the right and the long closed Barnwell Junction station just visible through the trees Class 47 No 47.004 passes with the 11.30 Kings Lynn-Liverpool Street on 28 November 1981. *Michael J. Collins*

Below: Photographed passing manual signals at Coldham Lane, Cambridge is Class 31 No 31.230 of Old Oak Common with a special ECS train from Norwich to Cambridge Yard on 5 November 1981. *Barry J. Nicolle*

Onwards From Ely

Left: Several manually operated crossings have survived into the 1980s around Ely. Class 37 No 37.033 traverses a fine example as it approaches the station in seven degrees of frost on 8 December 1980 with the 09.30 Kings Lynn-Liverpool Street. *Michael J. Collins*

Above right: Passing the wooden station buildings and awnings at Littleport is the 16.00 Kings Lynn-Liverpool Street on 15 April 1981 with Class 37 No 37.092 at the head. *Michael J. Collins*

Right: Approaching Downham Market from the south is Class 37 No 37.103 with the 07.34 Cambridge-Kings Lynn on 11 May 1982. The first passenger train of the day from Liverpool Street does not arrive at Kings Lynn until mid-morning and this working serves to bring a locomotive and coaches to the terminus in order to form an early up working. *Geoff Pinder*

Below: With hoar frost clinging to the sleepers Class 47 No 47.014 approaches Downham Market from the north with the 11.35 Kings Lynn-Liverpool Street. Until 1981 the station was known as Downham but the name was changed at the request of the local council. *Michael J. Collins*

Bottom: Although all present passenger services to Kings Lynn are air-braked, occasionally vacuum sets have to be substituted to allow maintenance of the former. On one such occasion Class 37 No 37.090 thunders past Denver Junction with the 08.35 Liverpool Street-Kings Lynn service on 28 April 1982. The line to Abbey and Wissington sugar factory can be seen diverging on the left. *Barry J. Nicolle*

Above: About to leave Kings Lynn with the 15.30 service to Liverpool Street is Class 37 No 37.115. The station, visible adjacent to the coaches, once boasted services to destinations all over East Anglia, but is now bereft of all trains except those to Cambridge and London. *Brian Morrison*

Left: An evocative winter time picture of an unidentified Class 37 about to leave Kings Lynn with the 13.25 train to Liverpool Street. *Peter Dobson*

Maritime Services: Freight to the East Anglian Ports

By far the majority of the freight traffic running in East Anglia is generated by the most vigorous ports within the region: at Harwich, Ipswich and Felixstowe in the east, and Tilbury in the south. These four ports have become nodal points in the Air Brake Network (ABN) and Freightliner routes currently being promoted by BR. The number of such services using East Anglian rails has been increasing in the 1980s and making the study of such services very difficult since train workings are constantly changing in response to customer demands and traffic conditions.

Throughout the 1980s the privately owned port of Felixstowe, under the auspices of the Felixstowe Dock and Railway Company, has been breaking records in terms of annual tonnages handled. Trade with our EEC partners has also enabled Harwich to develop as an outlet for imports and exports under the 'Sealink' banner and other independent enterprises. Therefore, both of these ports have been feeding considerable international traffic into the ABN and freightliner networks. The massive 'VTG Ferrywagons' and other continental vehicles form an increasing proportion of such trains and have become an everyday sight in East Anglia during the 1980s. Trains fan northwards via Bury St Edmunds and March and radiate southwards through London and via the North London Line.

An interesting ABN 'Speedlink' service featured in the 1981/82 working timetable illustrating the current BR thinking is the 15.50 Ipswich-Paisley. Surprisingly the train originates back at Chelmsford where four or five air-braked vans are collected from Rowntree's distribution centre and are worked forward as the 12.36 (Saturdays Excepted) to Ipswich Yard. The vans are then worked to March at the booked time of 15.50. Meanwhile a locomotive has worked from March depot along the single track freight only branch to Wisbech to collect further empty vans from a local pet food distributor. At March East Yard they are combined with the vans from Chelmsford and worked onwards to York where the Rowntree vans are detached. The Wisbech vans continue to Paisley. Clearly, flexibility also exists for attachment of further vans at other points on the route according to the dictates of demand and customer requirements.

Felixstowe is one of the UKs major deep sea container ports and during 1981 container traffic movement through the docks increased by over 40% to a new record of 348,930 boxes of which about 20% arrived by rail. Freightliner vehicles are marshalled into more or less permanent sets of five flats and during early 1982 the rail freightliner formations in and out of Felixstowe were as follows:

Outwards
1 Four sets, one each to Stratford/Leeds/ Glasgow and Holyhead on the Felixstowe-Willesden service.
2 Four sets, one each to Trafford Park/Swansea/ Birmingham and Garston on the Felixstowe-Stratford service.
3 Four sets all to Coatbridge.
4 Four sets, two destined for Trafford Park, and one each to Garston and Aintree on the Felixstowe-Trafford Park working.

Inwards
1 Four sets all from Coatbridge.
2 Four sets, one from Aintree, one from Birmingham and two from Garston on the Garston-Felixstowe working.
3 Three sets from Trafford Park and one set from Glasgow on the Trafford Park-Felixstowe service.

4 Four sets, one each from Leeds/Swansea/
   Holyhead and Stratford on the Stratford-
   Felixstowe service.

These timetabled workings are frequently swelled by
additional traffic running as required on special
schedules. Services to and from Felixstowe are
frequently loaded to 1,000 tonnes and during spring
1982 a record load of 1,400 tonnes was recorded on
the outward Trafford Park train.

Traffic has now reached the point where
Felixstowe is in desperate need of a second container
terminal. During winter 1981 Ipswich Lower Yard
was frequently being used as an overspill depot for
freightliner traffic from Felixstowe, the containers
being unloaded by a mobile crane. Sidings at
Stowmarket were also being used for such traffic. In
January 1982 it was announced that the Government
had agreed to give the Felixstowe Dock Company a
£1.3 million grant towards the cost of a second
container terminal. The news was received with
some disappointment, however, because the
company was only offered 40% (instead of the 50%
requested) of the £3.5 million cost of a four track
terminal and nothing towards the £1 million cost of
a new line linking the terminal to the Felixstowe
branch via a new spur near Trimley station. Failure
to build the new line will cause serious congestion
because trains to and from the new terminal will
have nine level crossings in the dock complex to
negotiate in order to reach the existing line.

Even at present the branch poses many
operational problems for freight trains because it is
single track and somewhat steeply graded. This
means that trains need at least Class 47 traction and
the heaviest workings require two Class 37s working
in multiple.

Ipswich has its own container facilities at Griffin
Wharf which is reached by a short spur diverging
from the GE main line at Halifax Junction. North of
the station, Ipswich Yard is a scene of much
shunting and splitting of freightliner trains being a
convenient mid-way point between Harwich and
Felixstowe. Trains heading north from Felixstowe
usually stop at this point either to run the engine
round the train or to obtain a fresh locomotive from
the stabling point. Ipswich itself is served by its own
container service to Trafford Park, Manchester.

Harwich has regular freightliner and ABN links
with distant destinations. It has freightliner links
every weekday with Halewood (Liverpool) and
Ripple Lane and is particularly associated with the
import and export of Ford Motor Company
products. Their distinctive blue containers carried as
block loads on company trains have become a
familiar sight within the region. In addition Harwich
has made the handling of motor vehicles one of its
specialist traffics. The Parkeston Quay-Mossend
services are frequently composed of 'Cartics' filled to

'47s' on Freightliners

**Below: Working down a rather arborial stretch of the
Harwich branch with a set of five loaded freightliner flats is
Class 47 No 47.004 recorded leaving Mistley during Spring
1980.** *Michael J. Collins*

capacity with cars heading north to Scotland with occasional large pieces of agricultural machinery conveyed on bogie-flats. This flow is supplemented by various special car trains which run on an 'as required' basis to and from vehicle manufacturing or distribution points at Bordesley (near Solihull), Dorridge (Birmingham) and Wrenthorpe (Wakefield).

In addition ABN services run from Parkeston to Sighthill, Millerhill, Bathgate, Bescot, Edge Hill and Tyne Yard, swelling the freight flow through East Anglia with a variety of merchandise. During March 1982 a new air-brake service was instituted from Parkeston to Warrington (Arpley Sidings) with a balancing return Warrington-Whitemoor service in order to cope with a freight flow newly identified by the operating authorities. With this kind of operating flexibility the future for air-braked traffic from and to the ports of East Anglia looks bright throughout the 1980s and beyond.

Above: Class 47 No 47.162 brings a heavy load of the blue liveried Ford Motor Co containers up the GE main line near Boreham forming the 16.30 Harwich (Parkeston Quay)–Halewood company train on 19 May 1980. *Michael J. Collins*

Below: Leaving Ipswich Lower Yard and crossing the River Gipping is Class 47 No 47.017 with the Ipswich–Trafford Park freightliner on 15 June 1982. Large locomotives are seldom seen on this branch, most workings being in the hands of the Colchester based '03s'. *John Day*

Above: With a 'Sealink' ship in the background Class 47 No 47.116 arrives at Parkeston Quay with a special Ipswich-Harwich freightliner working on 4 September 1981. *Brian Morrison*

Right: Working hard on the ascent of Belstead Bank is Class 47 No 47.579 *James Nightall GC* with the 10.27 Felixstowe-Willesden freightliner on 20 July 1982. The photograph was taken just after the infamous ASLEF dispute of 1982 and the load has been reduced to just one container situated behind the locomotive. *Michael J. Collins*

English Electric Power

Above: A Leeds–Tilbury freightliner is eased through Barking station on a dull 20 March 1982 headed by Class 37 No 37.057 and 37.060 working in multiple. *Michael J. Collins*

Below: An up Saturday morning air-braked freight for Harwich (Parkeston Quay) consisting of a set of five loaded container flats plus assorted air-braked vehicles is taken across the fens near Ely by Class 37 No 37.041 on 13 March 1982. *Michael J. Collins*

Above: Double heading on the GE main line is uncommon but a few of the Felixstowe freightliner workings are heavy enough to justify the use of the combined 3,500hp of two Class 37s. Nos 37.264 and 37.215 power the 11.15 Felixstowe-Stratford freightliner up the bank out of Witham on 14 April 1980.
Michael J. Collins

Left: This load of air-braked wagons is a mere toy for Class 40 No 40.057 as it takes the 23.35 Mossend-Parkeston Quay through Wrabness station on the Harwich branch on 3 September 1981.
Michael J. Collins

Right: This rare photograph depicts Class 40 No 40.097 on one of the few forays of the class on to the East Suffolk line during the 1980s. The train was a special working of empty container flats from Felixstowe which was captured on film passing Westerfield Junction on 24 September 1980. *Michael J. Collins*

Below: The 14.25 Parkeston Quay-Bathgate ABN was frequently rostered for Class 40 power during the early 1980s. No 40.192 hustles a load of northbound 'Cartics' along the Harwich branch at Mistley on 27 July 1981. *Michael J. Collins*

Below right: When the planned redevelopment of Ipswich station takes place during the mid-1980s this interesting roof level iron work will disappear. Class 40 No 40.185 passes with the 10.09 (Mondays only) Whitemoor-Parkeston on a snowy 19 December 1981. *Michael J. Collins*

Shunter Duties

Above: The Felixstowe Dock & Railway Company has its own ex-BR shunter for use within the dock system. Fresh from overhaul at Swindon Works, No D3489 Colonel Tomline was photographed sporting light green livery as it shunted 'Speedlink' air-braked vans within the dock complex on 1 September 1980.
Michael J. Collins

Left: Shunting vans for the continent on to a Sealink ship at Harwich Town Quay is dual-braked Class 08 No 08.530 on 6 January 1982. *Michael J. Collins*

Left: An unusual photograph of Class 03 No 03.196 shunting on the Ipswich Dock branch with the sailing barge 'Gladys' in the foreground and a more modern vessel behind. The forays of BR shunting locomotives into Ipswich Docks are becoming less common as the 1980s proceed. *Ian P. Cowley*

Below left: With the River Stour estuary in the background Class 08 No 08.767 was photographed bringing air-braked vans from a special munitions train from Carlisle up the steep gradient of the Mistley Quay branch during July 1982. *Michael J. Collins*

Serving the North

Above: Class 45s are very rare south of Ipswich on the GE main line but on 14 August 1981 No 45.010 was recorded approaching Manningtree with the 23.53 Mossend-Parkeston air-braked freight. *Michael J. Collins*

Left: This extraordinary load of three 'Algeco' tanks and a VTG Ferrywagon was photographed on the GE main line at Brantham approaching from the Whitemoor direction on 22 June 1981 hauled by Class 47 No 47.130. *Michael J. Collins*

Left: Many of the GE lines were built cheaply following the contours of the land as illustrated by this photograph of Class 37 No 37.050 between Elmswell and Thurston. The train is the 15.50 ABS Parkeston Yard-Arpley Sidings (Warrington) of 3 June 1982, a new service introduced during that year.
Michael J. Collins

Above: The 14.55 Parkeston Yard-Mossend ABS was formed of refrigerated 'Inter-Frigo' vans and VTG Ferrywagons as it was recorded approaching Mistley during August 1980 hauled by Class 31 No 31.154 on this occasion. *Michael J. Collins*

Right: The 21.24 Coatbridge-Felixstowe freightliner passes Claydon on the GE main line with Class 47 No 47.434 in charge on 3 October 1981. *John C. Baker*

General Freight Services

There is a variety of freight traffic traversing East Anglian lines outside the scope of the previous chapter. Much of this traffic runs outside the Air Brake Network and Freightliner 'modern image' services to and from the ports but some freight trains may be observed conveying odd air-braked wagons. These are likely to have vacuum pipes fitted so that they can travel in the older type services for incorporation into an ABN train later in their journey. This will soon become an outdated practice, however, because, as elsewhere, the East Anglian operating authorities are encouraging customers to move freight in block load trains. The modern trend is for these trains to be formed entirely of air-brake fitted vehicles, many being privately owned or leased by the customer from a third party.

This means that uniform trains of almost identical vehicles are becoming increasingly common in East Anglia during the 1980s.

East Anglia is frequently regarded as an essentially agricultural area and it is therefore surprising that so little of the rail traffic is generated by the farming community. In the past, sugar beet traffic to factories within the area was significant but rationalisation within the British Sugar Corporation has resulted in factory closures and a serious decline in the amount carried by rail in the 1980s. This decline is further manifested by the absence of limestone traffic, a raw material which is needed as part of the refining process.

Seed potatoes transported from Scotland also provided appreciable traffic flows to agricultural distribution centres such as Ely and Chelmsford. This commodity has now largely been lost to road haulage in response to BR's loss of interest in single wagon load traffic unless it can be incorporated into an existing ABN 'Speedlink' service.

The growing of grain is an agricultural speciality of the East Anglia area and several large storage depots within the region retain their rail connections. In particular, the depots at Chettisham, north of Ely, and one at Newmarket have regular flows to Whitemoor for onward transit to Scotland. The older type of four-wheel vacuum braked grain hoppers are gradually being phased out on these services to be replaced by the use of air-braked 'Polybulk' bogie wagons. This enables such consignments to be incorporated within the growing ABN 'Speedlink' services currently being encouraged by BR.

The growing ranks of ABN services have had their effect on the freight scene in East Anglia by instigating the virtual demise of the vacuum braked or unfitted mixed goods. Trains of this type have dwindled almost to the point of non-existence, reducing the importance of marshalling yards, because modern ABN services seldom need shunting. Parts of Whitemoor yard, March, were taken out of use and lifted during 1982 and closure of this famous centre in the near future looks inevitable.

The lion's share of general freight traffic traversing East Anglia during the 1980s is related to the natural resources and pockets of industry within the region. For several years appreciable quantities of sand from Middleton Towers (on the former Dereham line near King's Lynn) have been hauled by rail via the GN/GE joint line to Doncaster for use in the Northern glass industry. Until recently these trains have been running in formations of vacuum-braked hoppers but in 1982 a rake of air-braked hoppers was introduced heralding a transformation of these workings. Further sand pits at Stanway, south of Colchester, have their output carted by road to Marks Tey where daily services run to Mile End or Acton. A similar train runs from Fen Drayton (on the truncated Cambridge-St Ives branch) to King's Cross Goods and is the only remaining regular traffic on the branch which has survived into the 1980s.

Section 8 grants from the government have transformed sleepy sidings into busy freight centres almost overnight. In particular they have brought further aggregate traffic in the form of stone arriving in the area. Modern unloading facilities have been installed at Kennett, near Newmarket, and Barham, near Ipswich. To serve them, regular fully fitted air-braked trains run from Mountsorrel, near Leicester, and Westbury, Wiltshire. Similar trains run to Trowse, near Norwich also from Mountsorrel. This group of services has brought variety of traction to East Anglia in the form of pairs of Class 25s and more recently single Class 45s.

Coal traffic has seriously declined in recent years due to the reduction in domestic consumption and conversion to North Sea Gas. The one time procession of coal trains from the North via Whitemoor to Temple Mills has receded to the point where, in 1982, such traffic runs only on an 'as required' basis. Cement works within the region have regular deliveries of coal; the Barrington Cement Co's works at Foxton, on the Royston line, having a frequent consignment from Thoresby Colliery. The Blue Circle plant at Claydon, Ipswich has a regular service from the Chesterfield area. In addition, of course, finished and semi-finished cement is hauled by rail to and from each works

periodically. Domestic coal traffic is hardly significant in the 1980s but is still carried on a wagonload basis by such services as the daily Norwich-Yarmouth goods. This occasionally produces the rare spectacle of coal wagons being hauled in company with loaded freightliner flats.

Tank trains conveying large quantities of oil related products in 'block loads' regularly traverse the East Anglia region. These have become particularly associated with oil refineries on the LTS lines which serve industrial Thameside. Oil products flow through the area to and from South Humberside or the Teeside area to Ripple Lane for onward shipment to local refineries. Various oil

The Mixed Goods

Below: This mixed array of hoppers and other vehicles was photographed on 13 November 1981 approaching Great Chesterford on a Whitemoor-Temple Mills freight with Class 45 No 45.013 supplying traction. Class 45s are not unknown south of Cambridge but are far from common.
Colin J. Marsden

sidings within the area add to the traffic and North Sea Oil condensate is transported from North Walsham, on the Sheringham branch, to Harwich (Parkeston Quay). The sidings associated with the Cambridge based Ciba-Geigy Company at Whittlesford and Duxford generate regular chemical consignments, also transported in tanks.

Local demands for fertiliser used by the farming community is catered for by rail services to depots all over East Anglia from the UKF plant at Ince, Greater Manchester. One such working brings the only surviving regular freight train on to the Braintree branch with a load of 'Palvans' arriving most weeks travelling by a circuitous route via Syston, March and Ipswich.

With two existing nuclear powered reactors in the area at Sizewell (served by a branch from the East Suffolk Line) and Bradwell (served by the Southminster branch) the Central Electricity Generating Board is a respected BR customer. Spent and active nuclear rods are transported to and from Sellafield, Cumbria, for processing despite the activities of some conservation pressure groups and the 'anti-nuclear' lobby.

Following the withdrawal from collection and delivery the BR express and premium parcels service has been greatly reduced throughout the country. This has been reflected in East Anglia where few parcels trains now run. The 'Red Star' service, however, has been retained and will be expanded and special trains for the conveyance of **mail still**

continue to serve the requirements of the Post Office. An appreciable number of such trains emanate from Peterborough to Liverpool Street and vice versa with the possibility of onward shipment to a variety of northern destinations from Peterborough. Such trains run either 'directly' via Cambridge whilst some take the longer route via Ely, Bury St Edmunds and Ipswich. Continental destinations for mail are catered for by a direct Liverpool Street-Harwich service. The 1981 timetable saw the introduction of a new Southend Victoria to Manchester via Liverpool Street van train which was organised as a joint venture between the Post Office and BR carrying up to 8,000 mail bags per trip. The route is via Peterborough, Nottingham, Derby, Sheffield and the Hope Valley and replaced an aircraft service from Southend.

The BR operating authorities are sometimes quick to capitalise on special traffic by enterprising use of resources and this is particularly true in East Anglia. During the summer of 1981 an experimental tank train ran for six weeks from Chard Junction to Stowmarket conveying surplus milk from the West Country in order to cover a shortage in East Anglian dairies. The last train of empty milk trains left Stowmarket for Chard in October 1981. Five trains ran each way per week and including the trial run the train ran on 31 occasions. It is through capturing this kind of traffic that non-maritime traffic flows will survive in East Anglia into the late 1980s and beyond.

Right: Running alongside the 'New Cut' — one of the Broadland rivers — at Haddiscoe is Class 31/4 No 31.407 in charge of the 16.17 Lowestoft-Norwich freight on 6 April 1982. This working returns the morning newspaper van to Norwich plus any odd loads to hand which on this occasion included some CCE vehicles. *Michael J. Collins*

Above: This interesting train contains a mixture of coal wagons and freightliner vehicles plus a solitary steel flat. The working is the 08.58 Norwich–Yarmouth freight service which runs as a Class 7. The ensemble was photographed passing Wensum Junction on 15 April 1982.
Michael J. Collins

Below: Class 20s have made occasional forays into East Anglia during the 1980s and here Nos 20.016 and 20.163 leave Whitemoor with the 16.10 Whitemoor Yard to Temple Mills on 23 September 1981. The service was discontinued at the end of 1981 because of pathing difficulties at the London end. *Barry J. Nicolle*

Below: A really mixed load on this freight for Whitemoor photographed leaving Norwich on 30 May 1980 behind

Class 31 No 31.325. The Norman Keep of Norwich Castle is visible above and right of the brake van. *Michael J. Collins*

Coal Traffic

Right: With heavy frost hanging from the trees Class 45 No 45.013 leaves Cambridge with a Temple Mills bound train including a considerable amount of coal on 10 December 1981.
Kim Fullbrook

Above: Withdrawn at the beginning of the 1980s was the Ipswich-Melton coal train which traversed the southern end of the East Suffolk line. The photographer was fortunate to be able to record one of the last workings, hauled by Class 37 No 37.081, photographed passing Woodbridge with the empties. *John C. Hillmer*

Left: In recent years Class 25s have been extremely rare south of Cambridge, but in July 1980 No 25.123 was caught bursting from the south portal of Audley End Tunnel with coal from Whitemoor to Temple Mills. *Michael J. Collins*

Right: Class 44s used to penetrate regularly from Toton to March on coal trains right up to their ultimate demise. Here, one of the last visits by a class member was recorded on 30 October 1980 when No 44.008 *Pen-y-Ghent* headed back to Toton via Peterborough with a brake van after stabling a coal train in Whitemoor Yard. *Michael J. Collins*

Below right: Claydon cement works, near Ipswich, consumes 62,000 tonnes of coal per annum from the Chesterfield area. The coal is worked in on the 09.10 Ipswich Goods–Claydon. It has to stop for the engine to run round and then proceeds 'wrong line' into the works. Class 47 No 47.162 was photographed completing this manoeuvre on 20 August 1982. *Michael J. Collins*

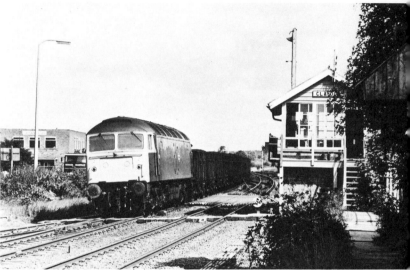

Flyash and Stone

Left: During the 1980s stone trains from Mountsorrel and Westbury have become almost daily events. Unloading the 09.48 Tuesdays and Thursdays only working from Mountsorrel is Class 45 No 45.074 photographed at Kennet (Redland Siding) near Newmarket on 27 April 1982. *John C. Baker*

Left: Sometimes the Kennet stone train is extended to serve Barham siding near Ipswich. A photographer was on hand to record Class 45 No 45.020 at Barham terminal with a working from Mountsorrel on 7 September 1981.
Ian P. Cowley

Centre left: Stone is also delivered to Barham sidings from Westbury, Wiltshire. In this picture the returning empties are hoisted up Belstead Bank by No 47.136 heading the 10.32 Tuesdays, Wednesdays and Thursdays Barham–Westbury Down Yard on 20 July 1982.
Michael J. Collins

Below: Flyash disposal is a problem for East Midlands power stations and it has to be taken far and wide for tipping. Heading north on the GN/GE Joint line at Spalding on 8 May 1982 is Class 47 No 47.209 with a long load of the 'Presflo' wagons used for this traffic.
Michael J. Collins

Right: This Fletton to Toton flyash empties train with Class 56 No 56.063 at the head was firmly in East Anglian territory when photographed at Peterborough North on 22 May 1982. It will soon depart northwards along the Midland exit to leave the area.
Michael J. Collins

Sand Transit

Above: Sand traffic from quarries near Kings Lynn to glass works near Doncaster forms a significant traffic. Class 37 No 37.009 was photographed at Middleton Towers on the truncated remains of the branch to Swaffham on 15 April 1981. The charming station buildings which have not welcomed a passenger since September 1968 still remain.
Michael J. Collins

Above: The transit of sand has kept open a section of the former Cambridge-St Ives branch into the 1980s. Class 37 No 37.024 makes a fine sight passing the remains of Histon station with the 07.58 Fen Drayton-King's Cross Goods on **16 March 1982.** *Kim Fullbrook*

Below: One of the yard shunters watches as Class 37 No 37.283 prepares to propel a rake of loaded sand hoppers from Fen Drayton into Cambridge Up Yard on 21 September 1981. The locomotive is actually standing on the remains of the hump yard knuckle now out of use. *Barry J. Nicolle*

Right: A consignment of sand leaves
Marks Tey Yard nearly every weekday.
Here the 10.30 COY Marks Tey Yard–
Acton train prepares to leave with
Class 37 No 37.048 at the head on
17 August 1982. *Michael J. Collins*

Below: During 1982 new air-braked
wagons were introduced on certain of
the sand workings. An unidentified
Class 37 approaches French Drove box
on the GN/GE Joint line on 29 May 1982
with the 10.50 COY (Thursdays,
Saturdays Only) Belmont (Yorkshire) to
Whitemoor sand empties on 29 May
1982. *Kim Fullbrook*

Tank Trains

Left: The only regular freight traffic now remaining on the Sheringham branch is the 13.00 North Walsham-Harwich (Parkeston Quay) train of tanks conveying North Sea Oil condensate. The consignment was photographed being hustled along the branch near Salhouse by Class 47 No 47.006 on 15 April 1982. *Michael J. Collins*

Centre left: The 11.52 Norwich-Ripple Lane oil tanker train empties growls past Haughley Junction on 22 February 1982 hauled by Class 37 No 37.053. The line to Cambridge and Ely via Bury St Edmunds can be seen branching west by the single track chord in the foreground. *Michael J. Collins*

Bottom: These interesting continental tanks contain chemicals destined for the Ciba-Geigy plant at Duxford and are being shunted in the sidings at Whittlesford by Class 31 No 31.268 on 28 July 1981. Note the tractor on the right specially 'customised' for shunting in the absence of a locomotive.
Colin J. Marsden

Right: This photograph had to be included because it depicts the seldom photographed Grassmoor Junction box situated in the heart of the vast Whitemoor Yard. Class 47 No 47.303 heads down the GN/GE Joint Line with a special return empty train from Royston to Teesport on 27 April 1982.
Barry J. Nicolle

Below: A westbound oil train headed by Class 37 No 37.019 was recorded heading across the Essex marshes when leaving Thames Haven on 8 September 1982. *Kim Fullbrook*

Special Freight

Left: On the remains of the Aldeburgh branch, at the site of the former Leiston station, stands Class 37 No 37.044 photographed on 25 February 1982. Beyond is a nuclear flask which has been conveyed from Sellafield between two barrier vehicles. It is destined for the nearby nuclear power station at Sizewell to which it will be transported by road.
John Day

Left: This photograph of Class 37 No 37.171 crossing the Essex marshes on the Southminster branch near Althorne, emphasises the desolate and remote nature of the countryside. The train is a nuclear flask from Bradwell Power Station to Sellafield and was recorded on 19 August 1982. *Michael J. Collins*

Centre left: The Class 31/0s (known as 'Toffeeapples') only just survived into the 1980s before withdrawal. One of the last workings for No 31.004 was this train of steel rod which it has brought from the port of Mistley to sidings at Witham where it was photographed on 5 September 1980. *Michael J. Collins*

Below: An astonishing load of two concrete bridge sections which formed part of Hills Road Bridge, Cambridge, is taken through March East Junction as an 'out of gauge' special by Class 37 No 37.034 on 17 May 1980. *Michael J. Collins*

Below: During summer 1981 a special service conveying milk from Chard Junction to Stowmarket ran for some weeks. Here the returning empties negotiate Bentley Bank on 26 August 1981 with Class 31 No 31.286, of Bristol Bath Road, in charge. *Michael J. Collins*

Block Load Freights

Left: Forming an air-brake network feeder service is this train of 'Speedlink' vans photographed at Wisbech with Class 40 No 40.078 about to couple up on 19 September 1980. The vans will be conveyed to March to be attached to the Ipswich-Paisley (Underwood) ABS service. *Michael J. Collins*

Below left: Class 37 No 37.020 was photographed to the south of Soham with the 15.52 (Saturdays Excepted) Ipswich-Paisley (Underwood) ABS service on 11 May 1982. *Barry J. Nicolle*

Left: The Chelmsford–Ipswich air braked van train speeds along the GE main line near Hatfield Peverel with Class 37 No 37.171 in charge on 27 July 1980. *Michael J. Collins*

Centre left: On the single track section Class 37 No 37.171 powers the 13.20 freight conveying empty grain wagons for Cambridge away from the station at Newmarket. Two vacuum piped bogie 'Polybulk' wagons and eight four-wheeled vacuum braked hoppers form the load. *Chris Burton*

Below: Passing Elsenham, on the Cambridge main line, is this train of empty 'Cartics' headed by Class 47 No 47.006 during June 1980. Note the staggered platforms and manual signalling still surviving at this rural station. *Michael J. Collins*

Cross-Country Passenger Services

This chapter focuses on the passenger services traversing East Anglia metals which are not aimed at travel to and from London. Possibly the 'prime mover' of these trains in terms of numbers of passengers carried, is the family of services spearheaded by the Norwich-Birmingham locomotive-hauled service which appeared in its present form in May 1977. At this time it was announced as an 'Inter-City' service but to this day the BR map issued with the passenger timetable shows the route as a thin line denoting 'other services'.

The pattern of services consists of five all the year round trains in each direction between the two cities, with an additional Birmingham-Norwich train running as a DMU in high summer. On Sundays the service is restricted to three services each way. A departure from the usual practice in the 1982/83 passenger timetable was the extension of certain of these services to Yarmouth on a permanent basis rather than for a few weeks during the peak holiday season. An improvement to these services during the 1980s was the addition of 'micro-buffets' which were far better than the rather basic facilities of the three car DMUs which handled these trains through the 1970s. It is a shame that more recently some trains have been running without this facility again.

The services to Birmingham use the 'Breckland' line through Thetford to Ely but since the recasting of the service in 1977 the Ely stop was omitted. Trains now traverse the curious Ely North Loop to avoid the station and then travel onwards to Birmingham via March and Peterborough.

For much of the winter the 'Breckland' line goes to sleep, carrying only this rather infrequent Inter-City service plus the Ely-Norwich local trains; its slumbers are only briefly punctuated by the passing of trains. On Saturdays, for a few weeks in the summer, however, the line briefly awakens again with extra dated services from Great Yarmouth to Leeds, Sheffield, Newcastle, Derby, London (via Ely) and Manchester all using the route. Up to 1981 an additional service to Walsall also used the route but it was axed as an economy measure at this time and has not been reinstated. All of these trains, until quite recently, used the Wensum Curve at Norwich to avoid reversal at Norwich Thorpe but the Crown Point Depot being constructed adjacent to the line has meant that all through passenger trains to Yarmouth reversed during 1981 and 1982. At the western end of their journey these holiday trains have been booked to traverse the GN/GE joint line from March to Spalding but this practice will cease in 1983 because after protracted negotiations and legal wrangling BR confirmed closure of the route while this volume was being prepared. As a consequence all such traffic will be re-routed via Peterborough in future years.

A second family of locomotive hauled cross-country passenger services emanates from the Harwich (Parkeston Quay) to Peterborough route. The daily through Harwich-Manchester service is perhaps the most anachronistic and well known of these services. This remarkable train starts early in the morning at London (Thornton Fields), where it is stabled, and is worked down to Harwich ecs in the early hours to connect with the night boat. It then works to Manchester via Peterborough (where it connects with the 08.50 King's Cross-Leeds) then via Nottingham and Sheffield. At this point the train used to reverse and change engines but in 1982 an innovation occurred when the train began to be routed via Tapton Junction and Beighton Junction. By doing this Sheffield Midland could be approached facing south so that the train could travel onwards to Manchester via Dore West Junction and the Hope

Valley. It was found that this cut out an engine change and thus saved several useful minutes.

The return service leaves Manchester Piccadilly mid-afternoon and works back by the same route, to be stabled during the late evening in London for servicing. Facilities for maintenance and overnight preparation of the stock do not exist in Harwich at present. The same stock makes the return journey day in day out and the Harwich based buffet car attendants work the round trip. The train became diagrammed to be worked by ETH fitted locomotives from August 1981 and has been taking a Stratford allocated locomotive to the North every day for some years. The train does not run on Sundays but for a limited time in summer does run to Sheffield only. This gives a useful Sunday northbound service from Harwich for travellers arriving in the UK following continental holidays where arrangements necessitated travelling across Europe on the Saturday.

The 12.40 Harwich (Parkeston Quay) to Peterborough and balancing return working have been well known locomotive hauled workings on this cross-country route for some years. The start of the 1982/83 timetable saw the introduction of additional locomotive hauled diagrams on this route together with some retiming of services. The above mentioned train, for example, now starts half an hour earlier. Also a new locomotive hauled Cambridge-Birmingham and balancing return working was introduced at the same time to replace a service previously handled by a DMU. All of this

family of services were designed with a view to providing good connecting services at Peterborough for interchange to the fast High Speed Train services to the North and Scotland.

Several cross-country passenger trains, such as the majority of the Cambridge-Peterborough services and the Ipswich-Cambridge trains utilise DMU stock. Other services entail much longer mileages in these machines for passengers. In the 1982/83 passenger timetable a new Ipswich-Spalding service was advertised — albeit only one train in one direction, and was diagrammed for a DMU set. The train had existed previously but was not advertised as a through working. For several years an early morning Bishop's Stortford-Norwich train has run using usually a five-car DMU set

'Birmingham Bound'

Below: Loaded to seven vehicles is the 13.16 Norwich-Birmingham service seen passing March West Junction on 27 May 1980 with Class 31 No 31.161 in charge. The signalbox above the rear coach is now closed and is a derelict and vandalised ruin. *Michael J. Collins*

throughout. The Ely-Norwich stopping service is still handled by DMUs for a through journey time of well over an hour. Although refurbished sets are increasingly making appearances on these services in the 1980s the stark contrast between them and the air-conditioned Inter-City image of the media advertisement can do little to promote travel on these trains during the remainder of the 1980s. The ancient Mark 1 rakes used on most of the locomotive hauled services until October 1982 must have had a similar effect. The East Anglian cross-country

services have been under-capitalised for years, although the introduction of electrically heated Mark 2 coaches on the locomotive hauled services during 1982 has been a modest improvement. Such gains are minimal, however, when the poor state of much of the track precludes any major acceleration of services. It is understood that so much investment is required to bring these services up to the modern BR image that closure is a distinct possibility on some routes. It is to be hoped that finance can be found.

Above: When Class 31s fail in Midland territory the operating authorities are sometimes pressed into substituting a Class 25. One such occasion was on 1 May 1982 when the 08.05 Birmingham-Norwich was recorded passing Stonea Box in the fens behind No 25.042. *John C. Baker*

Right: Diving under the GN Edinburgh main line on the exit to Peterborough is Class 31 No 31.208 hauling the 08.05 Birmingham-Norwich on 13 February 1982. *Michael J. Collins*

Left: One of the early disc fitted Class 31s No 31.107 hustles the 10.50 (Saturdays Only, Summer Dated) Yarmouth-Birmingham train through Wymondham on 29 May 1982.
Michael J. Collins

Harwich for the Continent, Peterborough for the North

Centre left: A substantial number of cross-country trains originate at Harwich (Parkeston Quay) to enable connections to be made with ships arriving from continental embarkation points. Class 37 No 37.102 prepares the stock of the 12.40 to Peterborough at Parkeston Quay on 18 June 1981.
Michael J. Collins

Below: Threading the Suffolk countryside at Elmswell is Class 31 No 31.249 heading the 12.40 Harwich (Parkeston Quay)-Peterborough service on 22 February 1982. *Michael J. Collins*

Above: The 07.17 Harwich (Parkeston Quay)-Manchester boat train still had many miles to travel when it was photographed at Bury St Edmunds on 17 October 1981 with No 47.525 in charge. *Michael J. Collins*

Right: An incredible event occurred on 23 November 1981 when Class 45 No 45.107 worked throughout to Parkeston on the return 15.15 Manchester-Harwich boat train. The booked locomotive had failed further north and the photographer was present at Ipswich to record the scene. *Ian P. Cowley*

Below right: Although the first vehicle is a non-passenger carrying GUV the train is the 16.38 Peterborough-Harwich (Parkeston Quay). The train was photographed at Ipswich with Class 31 No 31.418 in charge on 28 January 1982. *Michael J. Collins*

Left: The 16.45 Norwich–Peterborough train passes Stonea, behind Class 37 No 37.092 on 17 May 1980. In subsequent timetables this train was extended to serve stations onwards to Birmingham. *Michael J. Collins*

Below: Coming off the single line section at Soham on a wet 12 June 1982 is Class 31 No 31.262 hauling the 08.18 Peterborough–Ipswich service, one of the new locomotive hauled trains introduced in the 1982/83 timetable. *Michael J. Collins*

DMU
Cross-Country

Right: Passing the splendid wooden signalbox at Whittlesea is the 11.30 Peterborough-Cambridge service in the care of Cravens Class 105 DMUs Nos 51260/56126 on 13 February 1982. *Michael J. Collins*

Below: Despite BR's 1980s style 'Inter-City' image quite substantial journeys are still undertaken by DMUs in East Anglia. With the freight only Great Ryburgh branch curving off to the right a five-car set comprising Class 101 and Class 105 DMUs passes Wymondham South Junction with the 07.40 Bishops Stortford-Norwich service on 29 May 1982. *Michael J. Collins*

Left: The Norwich-Ely service is in the hands of DMUs for the hour and a half journey stopping at all stations. A Class 101 set, in immaculate ex-works condition, forms the 10.18 Ely-Norwich pausing at Brandon on 14 August 1982. *Michael J. Collins*

Centre left: A new working introduced in conjunction with the 1982/83 passenger timetable was a 14.50 Ipswich-Spalding service running via Cambridge, March and Peterborough. A two-car Class 105 unit forms this service on 19 July 1982 and was photographed on the GE main line approaching Needham Market. *Michael J. Collins*

Below: A Class 101 three-car DMU trailing a parcels van forms the Sundays 18.23 Cambridge-Ipswich. The working was photographed passing Coldham Depot, Cambridge, on 9 May 1982. *Kim Fulbrook*

Right: The 11.15 (Saturdays Only, Summer Dated) Birmingham-Great Yarmouth service is usually worked by a DMU set recalling the Birmingham-Norwich services of the 1970s. Passing Brandon box with this train is a six-car Class 116 set with No M50062 leading on 14 August 1982. Note the unit number which was painted above the front left buffer of these machines during 1982. *Michael J. Collins*

Saturdays Only/Summer Dated

Above: Passing the fine GE canopy at Cantley station is Class 47 No 47.143 hauling the 13.46 (Saturdays Only, Summer Dated) Great Yarmouth-Leeds express on 26 July 1982. *Michael J. Collins*

Above: All does not appear well with Class 37 No 37.110 photographed passing Brundall Junction signalbox with the 08.55 Saturday train from Newcastle to Great Yarmouth on 19 June 1982. *Michael J. Collins*

Left: On summer Saturdays some additional Norwich–Birmingham services are extended to start from Great Yarmouth. Class 31 No 31.418 snakes over Reedham Junction with the 13.38 Great Yarmouth–Birmingham on a dull 19 June 1982. The line diverging to the right is to Lowestoft via the Reedham swing bridge. *Michael J. Collins*

Above: On the GN/GE Joint Line passing Murrow West signalbox is Class 31 No 31.253 hauling the Saturdays Only 15.23 Great Yarmouth-Sheffield on 20 June 1981. At this point the now closed and lifted Midland & Great Northern Branch from Wisbech to Peterborough used to cross on the level. *Kim Fulbrook*

Below: The summer Saturday trains frequently bring non-boilered locomotives into passenger service. A Tinsley engine with boiler isolated, No 31.147 leaves Thetford with the 07.10 Chesterfield–Great Yarmouth summer dated train on 5 June 1982. *Michael J. Collins*

Multiple Working on the Breckland Line

Above: The 08.00 (Saturdays Only, Summer Dated) Walsall-Great Yarmouth express was a victim of the cuts in the 1981/82 timetable. The train was photographed traversing Thetford Forest at Santon Downham on 2 August 1980 hauled by Class 25s Nos 25.272 and 25.291. *Michael J. Collins*

Left: Cautiously rounding the Ely avoiding loop on 12 July 1980 are Class 25s Nos 25.125 and 25.132 heading the 08.35 Derby-Great Yarmouth holiday train. The flat scenery, so typical of fenland, is clearly evident in this picture. *Michael J. Collins*

Below left: An unusual Class 31/1 plus 31/4 combination photographed passing a fine semaphore signal at Lakenheath with the 13.46 Great Yarmouth-Leeds express on 12 June 1982. The locomotives are 31.115 and 31.407. *Michael J. Collins*

Above: The 08.04 Birmingham–Great Yarmouth is frequently strengthened to meet increased passenger demand on summer Saturdays. With 10 vehicles in tow Class 31s No 31.291 and 31.255 provide the traction on 5 June 1982 seen here accelerating away from Thetford. *Michael J. Collins*

Below: Although in 1982 the 08.33 (Saturdays Only, Summer Dated) Derby–Great Yarmouth service produced a variety of motive power including Class 25, 31, 37 and 47s, only once did a pair of Class 20s (known locally as 'Ducks') make an appearance. On 28 August 1982 Class 20 Nos 20.160 and 20.136 make their way round the Ely avoiding loop near Queen Adelaide. *Barry J. Nicolle*

Branch Lines

The passenger branch lines of East Anglia have suffered in the past through closures and those that are open in the 1980s are only the skeletal remains of a once complex network. The majority of the branch lines which are still carrying passengers at the present time have the prime function of attracting custom to the Inter-City rail heads. A few lines in the south of the region have been upgraded, modernised and electrified to become commuter routes. The sad fact remains, however, that most East Anglian branch lines have suffered from years of lack of under capitalisation, and investment money is being used to merely keep trains running. On some lines the problem has become so acute that the phrase 'the crumbling edge of British Rail' has been coined and accurately describes the state of much of the branch line network.

During the Beeching era, the East Anglian branch lines were almost decimated and in the 1980s the stage has been reached where any further closures could well have serious repercussions on the Inter-City network through a fall-off in revenue; all the branch lines bringing in significant custom on to main line services.

There can be no doubt that the introduction of the 'Paytrain' concept in 1967 has saved the remaining East Anglian branch lines from closure. The Sheringham branch, for example, would certainly have been ripe for the axe but for the advent of the scheme.

As a result of East Anglia being an agricultural area the pattern of settlement tends to be very dispersed. Coupled with one of the highest levels of car ownership per head of population traffic is not easily attracted back from the roads. The problem is compounded by the low general level of wages in this part of the country. For these reasons it is difficult to forecast any dramatic change in loading levels of

East Anglian branches and the economic stringencies of the early 1980s have resulted in BR casting a critical eye over some of the rural branch lines, with a view to further cost cutting. The reduction in manning levels achieved by the 'Paytrain' concept in the 1960s may well have to be matched by a similar financial exercise in the 1980s to ensure the survival of many branches into the next decade. The state of the track and other items of fixed equipment is deteriorating rapidly on many of the branches and a heavy injection of capital in exchange for reduced manning levels looks to be a vital move.

The Wherry Lines
This is the name given by the publicity department of BR to the group of lines radiating eastwards from Norwich to Lowestoft and Yarmouth. These lines had the distinction of being among the first lines to be operated by DMUs under the modernisation plan of the 1950s.

The Lowestoft and Great Yarmouth line diverges from the GE main line at Thorpe Junction, just east of the main Norwich station, and retains double track throughout despite there being only a basic hourly interval service in each direction. Nearly all of the about 14 daily weekday trains from Lowestoft connect with Inter-City services at Norwich.

The trains are handled by the ubiquitous Cravens two-car Class 105 sets but some refurbished Metro-Cammell Class 101 three-car sets have been infiltrating on to the route. All but a few trains stop at all stations on the journey to Norwich but one train in the morning peak calls only at Oulton Broad North with a 'fast' run to Norwich.

The station at Lowestoft was rebuilt during 1961 and the wooden all-over roof has survived together with a bookstall and other amenities which remain open. This could well change, however, as the 1980s proceed because the station stands on a prime town centre site and it has been suggested that it could with advantage be moved back to allow for redevelopment.

Services from Norwich to Yarmouth have a choice of two routes: either branching from the Lowestoft Line at Brundall Junction and running via Acle or continuing to Reedham Junction and running via the anachronistic and isolated Berney Arms station situated in the Norfolk marshes. Both these routes to Yarmouth have surprisingly remained single track, resulting in severe congestion in summer when holiday extras boost the traffic. On weekdays in 1982/83 there were 18 local DMU operated services running between Norwich and Yarmouth. Added to these were a number of Birmingham-Norwich and London-Norwich locomotive hauled trains which extend to Yarmouth.

The Broads Line
This is the name given to the $30\frac{1}{2}$ mile long Norwich-Sheringham branch although in reality it only traverses the Norfolk Broads at the southern half of the route. The line is double track as far as Wroxham but beyond that point it is singled. From North Walsham onwards the line is worked as a passenger siding and all trains have to reverse at Cromer before following the last surviving passenger section of the Midland & Great Northern Joint Railway to reach Sheringham. The service is roughly one train every two hours in each direction connecting with Inter-City London arrivals and departures at Norwich but one peak morning and evening train works only as far as Cromer.

The East Suffolk Line
This line is now reduced to branch line status and is all that remains of a former main route which boasted expresses from London to Lowestoft and continuations to Yarmouth. It is surprising that the line still retains its double track into the 1980s because the timetable has been suitable for single line working for many years. It is believed that BR prefers to keep the double track in situ because, through years of underinvestment, the line is in very poor shape and two tracks reduce the wear received by any one individual line. In the 1982/83 passenger timetable the branch had only 10 DMU worked

services to Lowestoft from Ipswich. These are swelled by the daily up and down locomotive hauled train serving London direct running fast from Colchester. On summer Saturdays the line returns to a little like its former glories when an additional up and down through service is provided to cater for the additional loadings afforded by holiday traffic.

Threatened with closure in the past, the line was the very first 'Paytrain' route leading to the survival of the route into the 1980s. Recently BR have been investigating other ways of reducing costs on the line and it is clear that without substantial savings of fixed costs and equally substantial investment the survival of the branch beyond the 1980s appears to be in doubt.

Branches to Harwich and Felixstowe
Operated by DMUs the Felixstowe line is a single track branch from the East Suffolk line at Westerfield Junction. It threads a semi-circle for six miles around the Ipswich outskirts before following the northern bank of the River Orwell estuary to reach the prosperous port. There are three intermediate stations between Ipswich and Lowestoft surviving into the 1980s.

The line affords considerable operational problems because there is an ever growing freight traffic on the line which has to be fitted between passenger trains. The basic service consists of 10 return trains each way on weekdays with thee summer Saturday extras provided to cope with the enhanced business. About 8,000 passenger journeys per week are made on the branch in the summer peak. The line closes on Sundays for the duration of the winter from September to May but in summer a Sunday service of weekday frequency is maintained.

Running on the almost parallel southern bank of the River Orwell estuary is the double track Harwich branch. In effect services on this line form two separate entities; the boat train traffic to Harwich (Parkeston Quay) and the local services which run along the single line extension to Harwich Town. The branch line services connect at Manningtree with the Norwich semi-fasts which call there every two hours. One or two of the services are extended to run through to either Ipswich or Colchester and in the 1982/83 passenger timetable a rather odd Harwich Town-Stowmarket working exists. At present the line is semaphore signalled throughout beyond the junctions at Manningtree but is due to change to mas on completion of the Colchester resignalling scheme.

The Sudbury Branch

Sometimes known as the 'Stour Valley' line the single track branch diverges from the electrified Colchester main line at Marks Tey. It was once part of an extensive system which ran to Cambridge but the line now has to earn revenue from the passenger traffic from Sudbury and the intermediate villages to Colchester. The line has several times been threatened with closure and debate about its future, with occasional scares about imminent demise, continue in the 1980s. The line is probably the epitome of all the ills of East Anglian branch lines in that the infrastructure is life expired. Passenger facilities are basic at best, the 1,066ft long Chappel Viaduct, which consumed seven million bricks in construction, is visibly decaying; and passenger receipts are difficult to improve.

The basic weekday service from Sudbury is now 11 trains a day with an extra late evening train on Thursdays and Fridays only. In 1980/81 some trains were extended to run to and from St Botolphs station in an attempt to attract more shoppers' revenue because this station is more convenient for the town centre. Some other trains are extended to run to and from Ipswich because of stock servicing and stabling constraints. On Sundays the branch service is reduced to seven trains each way in summer. During the winter months Sunday train services on the branch do not start until after lunch with a consequent reduction to four trains each way. Passengers levels on all but the morning and evening peak services are very low; the survival of this branch beyond the 1980s must be in the balance.

'Inter-City Feeders'

Below: Weed infestation and decay at Sudbury, the terminus of a branch line which once extended to Cambridge. A Class 105 two-car DMU comprising unit Nos 56440/51279 arrives at the one remaining usable platform on the 18.03 service from Colchester North on 14 August 1982. Some services on the branch run to and from St Botolphs station (situated nearer to the centre of Colchester) in an attempt to attract shoppers' traffic. *Michael J. Collins*

Above: On the single track Felixstowe branch two Cravens Class 105 DMUs make a four-car set forming the 10.00 service from Ipswich. The ensemble was photographed near the site of the former station at Orwell on 5 June 1982. *Michael J. Collins*

Below: The GN/GE Joint line has been reduced to branch line status in recent years. A Class 111 two-car set with unit No E51541 leading approaches Spalding with the 10.31 Doncaster-Cambridge service on 29 August 1982. The train allows passengers to reach Inter-City services to Norwich and Birmingham at March and to London at Cambridge. *Michael J. Collins*

Above: Through the decorated entrance to Harwich Town station can be seen a two-car Cravens DMU set forming an afternoon working to Manningtree on 13 May 1981. This train will connect with Inter-City services to both London and Norwich at Manningtree. *Michael J. Collins*

Locomotive hauled on the Branches

Above: The Chippenham Junction–Cambridge line is operated almost entirely by DMUs on the Ipswich–Cambridge service. The 07.08 from Ipswich is extended to London and is usually formed of a locomotive and a rake of elderly Mark 1 coaches. In pouring rain Class 37 No 37.023 was recorded approaching Dullingham with the working on 12 June 1982.
Michael J. Collins

Above: On alternate winter Saturdays the 12.50 Cambridge-Ipswich ran during 1981/82 as a strenthened locomotive hauled set to convey local supporters to Ipswich Town FC matches. Class 31 No 31.236 leaves Newmarket with this train on 28 November 1981. *Michael J. Collins*

Right: Deputising for a failed DMU set is Class 37 No 37.092 photographed as it entered the passing loop at Acle station with the 17.50 Yarmouth-Norwich service composed of three Mark 1 coaches. *Michael J. Collins*

Above right: Clacton line services occasionally have to be locomotive hauled when the overhead electric current is switched off for maintenance. One such occasion was 7 March 1982 when Class 37 No 37.261 entered Clacton station with a re-timed train from Liverpool Street. *Michael J. Collins*

The East Suffolk

Above: Leaving Lowestoft with the 12.55 to Ipswich is a Class 105 twin-car unit on 6 April 1982. Notice the manual signalling still surviving and the splendid all over wooden roof of the station. *Michael J. Collins*

Below: The 07.22 Lowestoft-Liverpool Street and 17.00 down return train are booked for locomotive haulage. Here Class 37 No 37.116 pauses at Saxmundham on 6 April 1982 with the up morning train. The new down platform, beyond the signalbox, was opened in 1981 and spelled the end for the ornate canopy of the old platform. *Michael J. Collins*

Left: Passing the peeling paintwork of Beccles station is a four-car formation of Class 105 DMUs forming the 07.02 Ipswich-Lowestoft on 19 June 1982. *Michael J. Collins*

Centre left: Roaring through Halesworth with the 09.53 (Saturdays Only, Summer Dated) Liverpool Street-Lowesoft holiday express is Class 47 No 47.566 photographed on 15 August 1981. *Kim Fullbrook*

Below: Passing broads cruisers as it crosses the swing bridge at Oulton Broad South is the 09.04 Ipswich-Lowestoft comprising Class 105 DMUs Nos E56437 and E50384 on 6 April 1982. *Michael J. Collins*

Spokes from Norwich

Right: Leaving Cromer a Cravens two-car Class 105 DMU traverses the only remaining trackbed of the former Midland and Great Northern Joint Railway still open to passengers. The train is the 11.12 Sheringham-Norwich service photographed on 24 April 1982.
Michael J. Collins

Centre right: On the Sheringham branch the blue enamel signs once synonymous with Eastern Region stations have survived into the 1980s. Standing at the branch terminus is a Cravens Class 105 twin car DMU forming a morning train to Norwich on 24 April 1982.
Michael J. Collins

Left: Crossing the novel swing bridge at Reedham, Norfolk, which rotates on its central pivot to allow river traffic to pass, is the 11.24 Lowestoft-Norwich on 19 June 1982 formed by a two-car DMU. *Michael J. Collins*

Right: Although once familiar on services from the Midlands the Class 120 Swindon cross-country DMUs now only have one regular East Anglian working on an unbalanced summer Saturday service from Birmingham. No 50659 leads set No EP520 past Whitlingham Junction forming the 16.49 Yarmouth-Norwich service on 26 June 1982 while working back to home territory. *Michael J. Collins*

Top: Leaving Hoddiscoe is another DMU forming the 15.52 Norwich-Lowestoft photographed during April 1982. The signalbox on the horizon is a remnant of the former East Suffolk Beccles-Yarmouth branch which had its own station at Haddiscoe High Level. *Michael J. Collins*

Above: Passing the rather basic station facilities and splendid old signalbox at Buckenham is the 13.31 Norwich-Yarmouth local train formed by a ubiquitous Class 105 twin-car unit on 26 June 1982. *Michael J. Collins*

Locomotive, unit and rolling stock maintenance

Motive power depots either situated in East Anglia or having a large number of locomotives at work within the area are shown in Table 1 together with the position regarding locomotive allocations as at mid-May 1982

Table 1

East Anglian Motive Power Depots and number of traction units allocated

| Motive Power Depot | Number of locomotives allocated by classes | | | | | DMU car allocation |
	'03'	'08'	'31'	'37'	'47'	
Stratford Maintenance and Repair Depot	—	34	18	33	50	38
Ripple Lane Servicing Depot	No allocation					
Colchester Servicing Depot	3	12	—	—	—	—
Cambridge Maintenance Depot	—	10	—	—	—	15
March Maintenance Depot	2	18	43	25	—	—
Norwich Thorpe Maintenance Depot*	7	3	—	—	—	106
Totals	12	77	61	58	50	159

*Closed during late 1982 and duties taken over by Norwich Crown Point Depot.

All of these depots, with the exception of Norwich Thorpe, have purpose built facilities for the routine maintenance of diesel locomotives and diesel multiple-units. All of the depots are staffed around the clock, thus making it possible for traction unit maintenance to continue 24 hours a day.

The £7 million Crown Point multi-purpose depot at Norwich was completed in late 1982 and opened by Sir Peter Parker. It was an innovative scheme which became the maintenance base for diesel locomotives, Inter-City carriage stock sets, and diesel multiple-units needing attention within the Norwich area. All these activities are now taking place under the same roof within the same general area instead of the older system of providing quite separate facilities for the maintenance of different kinds of stock.

Locomotives from the East Anglian depots run considerable mileages on long, complicated diagrams taking them to all parts of the Eastern Region. Some diagrams take East Anglian machines to the Midlands, Western, Southern and Scottish regions with regularity.

Table 2

Weekday Locomotive Requirements — March Diesel Depot May 1982 (excluding shunters)

Class 37	Class 31
18 Dual Braked (4 non-boilered)	2 Dual Braked/Dual heat
2 Vacuum braked (non-boilered	8 Dual braked (1 non-boilered
	23 Vacuum braked (non-boilered)
Total: 20	*Total: 33*

The difference between the number of locomotives allocated to the depot at March (Table 1) and the number actually required for work (Table 2) is extremely small and thus some very efficient servicing work is demanded from depot staff. Most depots can undertake routine servicing work and can accomplish minor repairs and adjustment, but for major repairs to bogies or power units locomotives are usually sent to a main works or Stratford Diesel Repair shop. This depot can undertake very heavy and complex repairs including frame repairs, fire damage rectification, and has facilities for tyre turning. The depot also takes in work from all parts of the Eastern Region and when Class 55 'Deltic' repairs ceased at Doncaster Works in November 1981 the work was taken over by Stratford for the final few months of service. By late November 1981 several of the class were present, engines and other usable parts being removed, in order to keep the remaining 12 machines running.

In addition to the maintenance facilities listed in Table 1 stabling and/or fuelling facilities exist at the following locations:

Liverpool Street Station Fuelling Depot
Great Yarmouth Stabling Point
Lowestoft Stabling Point
Ipswich Fuelling Point
Cambridge Station Stabling Point
King's Lynn Fuelling Point

To the south of the East Anglia region large numbers of electric multiple units connected with the commuter services into London are maintained. The allocations are shown in Table 3.

Table 3

Electric multiple unit depots and number of units allocated May 1982

	East Ham EMU Depot	Ilford Electric MD	Clacton Electric TMD
Class 302	91	21	—
Class 305	—	71	—
Class 307	—	32	—
Class 308	9	15	20
Class 309	—	—	23
Class 312	—	—	20
Class 313	—	—	4
Class 315	—	61	—
Totals:	100	200	67

All of the three maintenance depots have modern facilities and can undertake extensive repairs and refurbishment work, such as bogie changes, power unit replacement etc. Until 1981 work at Clacton took place in rather outdated facilities in a two road shed about $\frac{1}{4}$ mile from the station but on 17 July 1981 the new Clacton Electric Traction Maintenance Depot, with modern facilities was brought into use. With further electrification programmed for East Anglian lines it seems likely that more similar installations will be opened in the future.

Locomotives at Depots and Fuelling Points

Below: Stratford Traction Maintenance Depot, in East London, services many of the locomotives at work in East Anglia. In this view taken on 1 June 1980 are Nos 46.050 (left) and 46.030 (right) undergoing bogie attention. Work proceeds with WR based DMU No W59491 (centre). Also on view is Class 47 No 47.311. *Michael J. Collins*

Right: Parked among the weeds at March Depot is an invader from the north in the form of Class 40 No 40.074 on 11 September 1982. A Class 47 can be seen behind and a pair of Class 20s lurk on the right. *Michael J. Collins*

Centre right: Standing outside Norwich Thorpe Maintenance Depot is the prototype Class 37 No 37.119 (formerly D6700) on 6 February 1982. Behind can be seen the former steam depot buildings and one of the former 'Toffeeapple' Class 31s used as a non-powered eth carriage pre-heater. *Michael J. Collins*

Below: Variety at Colchester Servicing Depot on 26 August 1980. On view are (from left to right) Class 31s Nos 31.160 and 31.164, Class 37 No 37.039, former Class 15 Locomotive No ADB968001 and Class 08 No 08.228. *Michael J. Collins*

Below: Ipswich no longer has an open maintenance depot or an allocation of locomotives. Significant numbers of engines still gather at the fuelling point alongside the station. On the night of 8 January 1982 Class 03 No 03.179 stands near the fuelling bay while a DMU receives its ration beyond.
Michael J. Collins

Carriage Stock and EMU Maintenance

Above: At Cambridge Maintenance Depot facilities for servicing carriage stock under cover exist in the former diesel shed. Class 08 No 08.052 deposits a couple of GUVs and a Mark 2 carriage in the depot with a Class 101 twin-car unit stabled in an adjacent road during May 1980.
Michael J. Collins

Above: A rake of nine eth coaches is marshalled at Yarmouth carriage sidings by Class 03 No 03.397 on 6 February 1982. Beyond is one of the eth pre-heaters which is used to warm the stock overnight. Stabling of rolling stock at Yarmouth will decrease when the new depot at Crown Point, Norwich, comes into use. *Michael J. Collins*

Below: At Shoeburyness large numbers of the LTS line EMUs are stabled in the extensive sidings. A line up of Class 302 units was photographed at this location on 20 March 1982. *Michael J. Collins*

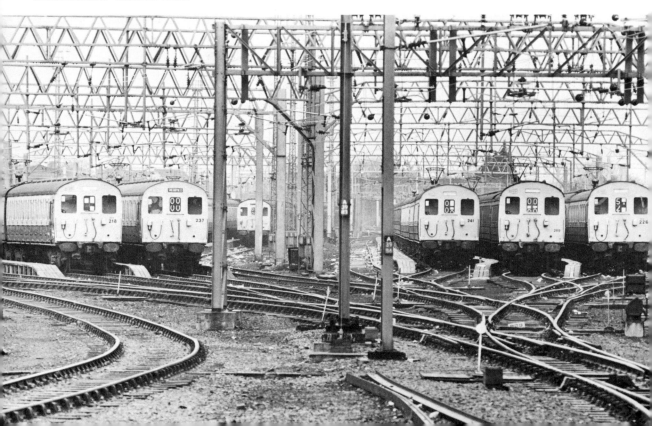

Above: Leaving the now redundant old electric depot at Clacton is Class 308 EMU No 147 on 20 April 1982.
Les Bertram

Left: Standing inside the modern facilities at the new electric traction maintenance depot at Clacton, opened during 1981, are two of the fast Class 309 units Nos 618 and 615 photographed during June 1982.
Michael J. Collins

Carriage pre-heaters

Above: When hauled stock is stabled overnight in the open unpowered pre-heaters are employed. ADB968015 (formerly Class 31/0 No 31.014) stands partially under cover at Norwich Thorpe Maintenance Depot on 6 February 1982. *Michael J. Collins*

Below: Some former Class 15 locomotives were converted for use as non-powered eth carriage pre-heaters at Colchester Servicing Depot. The jumper cable for connection to the carriage stock can be seen above the left buffer in this photograph of ADB968002 (formerly No D8237) at Colchester on 25 August 1980. *Michael J. Collins*

Commuter Services

Since the days of the Great Eastern 'jazz services', Liverpool Street has been associated with an intensive traffic from outer suburban destinations and this continues in the 1980s. High wages in Central London and electric multiple units running to fast schedules, with a good service frequency, have enabled commuters to consider a daily journey to work from much more distant parts than was previously possible. Inner suburban areas such as Enfield and Chingford have been supplemented by East Anglian towns such as Clacton, Colchester and Braintree as viable commuter destinations. At the time of writing, the price of an annual season ticket from Braintree to Liverpool Street is £916, which means that the East Anglian commuter area is perhaps restricted to higher wage earners. More and more employers, however, are giving workers assistance with season ticket purchase and therefore making longer journeys worthy of consideration.

At the beginning of the 1980s the EMU stock used on the majority of these services was beginning to show the effects of years of intensive use and under investment. Excepting 26 new Class 312 units, much of the equipment was beginning to reach the end of its planned life. Since then, during 1981/82, commuters have seen a large proportion of the stock refurbished. Improvements to the inside upholstery and layout of units was programmed in order to enhance passenger comfort and discourage vandalism. Major overhauls to traction equipment took place under a refurbishment programme in an attempt to achieve greater reliability. During 1980/81 the ageing Class 306 sliding door units were all withdrawn and replaced by the modern Class 315 units conforming to the new BR design image for this type of machine. These units have brought with them a new era of impeccable riding, good time keeping and smart appearance on the inner-suburban lines. This is in keeping with their excellent acceleration characteristics and internal decorative scheme, using up to date materials and design techniques. During 1981/82 this new machinery started to reach Southend Victoria on certain services.

The Essex town of Braintree has had considerable importance as a dormitory town and commuter base for some years but during the 1970s travel to Liverpool Street required a change of train at Witham. Electrification enabled through working from Liverpool Street and the 1981/82 passenger timetable featured a new through hourly semi-fast service. Regular all the year round Sunday trains on this route were introduced in 1982 after two years of trial running in summer only supported by financial guarantees by the local council.

Improvements on the Braintree branch allowed recasting of the Clacton trains enabling Clacton fasts to be accelerated by omitting the stop at Shenfield. It was unfortunate, however, that the sizeable contingent of commuters from the Clacton line were compelled to lose their on-train buffet facilities from 31 October 1980 because of alleged uneconomic levels of patronage. The last service to retain a buffet car was the 17.00 Liverpool Street-Clacton-on-Sea/Walton-on-Naze of that date. The extra space thus gained will be utilised in the form of increased seating accommodation which will be welcomed because custom on peak hour services is brisk. The 1982/83 passenger timetable saw the abandonment of the practice of attaching a four-car EMU to the Clacton-London trains at Thorpe-le-Soken, this being replaced by a connecting train on the five mile branch to Walton-on-Naze. The branch now has only one remaining through peak hour service to London and some summer dated Sunday services together with just one through local service to Colchester.

The Colchester-Clacton/Walton line has seen the appearance of four Class 313 units which were procured from the GN electrified area for work on the local stopping services running via St Botolphs. The new units were modified for use in the area by having the trip cocks and third rail current collection equipment removed because this machinery was only required on the tunnel section into Moorgate.

The LTS lines to Southend and Shoeburyness have enjoyed a frequent commuter service to Fenchurch Street over many years and still boasts an excellent service running virtually round the clock. Trains use one of two loops running via either Tilbury or Upminster, the pair of lines joining again at Pitsea. Some trains run via the Ockenden branch to reach the Essex coast.

The line to Southend Victoria also has a good service running via Shenfield. Passenger levels are swelled on daytime services by the considerable commuter traffic generated by the DMU operated 'New Essex' line from Southminster which joins at Wickford. The village of South Woodham Ferrers, which is served by the branch, is being expanded into a new town by the Essex County County Council, and is thus likely to generate further traffic as the 1980s proceed.

Commuter Services

Below: Class 305 four-car EMU No 505 stands under the magnificent arch at Liverpool Street before leaving with the 14.38 service to Bishops Stortford from Platform 10 on 3 July 1982. *Michael J. Collins*

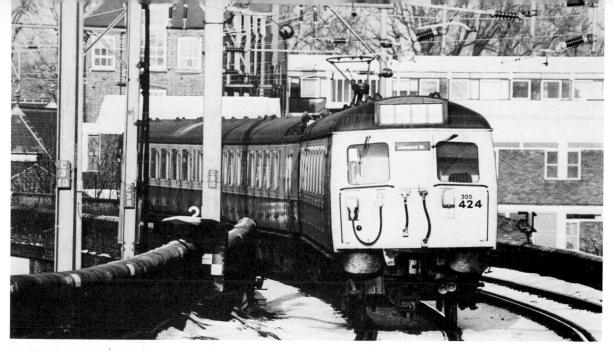

Above: Class 305 three-car unit No 424 takes the Southbury loop at Hackney Downs with a service from Liverpool Street to Cheshunt on 16 January 1982. *Michael J. Collins*

Left: Once the mainstay of inner suburban services from Liverpool Street were the Class 306 units, but they were all withdrawn from service by the end of 1981. Here two sets, Nos 051 and 011 descend Brentwood Bank with a Southend Victoria to Liverpool Street commuter train on 30 July 1980. *Michael J. Collins*

Below left: Replacements for the Class 306 units were the 315s, their design conforming to modern BR practice. Here an eight-car formation led by 315.812 approaches Ilford on an inner-suburban working on 3 July 1982. *Michael J. Collins*

Top: Besides carrying an appreciable flow of London bound commuters, the Clacton branch receives revenue from workers travelling to the Colchester area from the coast. Class 313 No 313.039 arrives at St Botolphs with a Clacton-Colchester stopping train on 22 August 1982.
Michael J. Collins

Above: Walton-on-Naze has a sizable contingent of commuters and in the 1982/83 timetable their needs were catered for by only one up and one down through train to London. In the days when the town had a through service to Colchester Class 308 No 138 was seen with the 16.06 train on 20 April 1981. At present most trains from here only go as far as Thorpe-le-Soken. *Les Bertram*

Above: Class 305 No 420 arrives at Hertford East forming a working from Liverpool Street. Note that the orignal signalbox was retained after modernisation and the searchlight type colour light signals add interest to the scene. *John Glover*

Left: The diesel worked Southminster branch has a significant commuter traffic despite the change of trains needed at Wickford. On 19 August 1982 a Class 116 set with No 50853 leading was photographed passing a delightful manual signal near Fambridge while forming the 09.28 Wickford–Southminster — despite the 'Stratford' destination blind! *Michael J. Collins*

Right: Unit number 302.301 forms the 13.10 Fenchurch Street-Shoeburyness via Upminster service as it runs into Thorpe Bay station on 20 March 1982. Note the beautiful station awnings which have survived well into the 1980s. *Michael J. Collins*

Centre right: Cross platform interchange on the LTS at Grays, Essex, with unit number 302.298 forming the 10.05 Fenchurch Street-Shoeburyness via Tilbury and 302.297 forming the 10.40 branch line service to Upminster via Ockenden on 20 March 1982. *Michael J. Collins*

Below: Class 308/2 units are equipped with Motor Luggage Vans (MLVs) and are intended to carry parcels, mail etc at off peak times when passenger space can be sacrificed. Unit 308.321 stands at Tilbury Riverside on 20 March 1982 with the MLV second vehicle from the front. *Michael J. Collins*

Passenger Specials

Footex/Adex/Mystex Excursions

To the uninitiated the above terms refer to advertised BR sponsored special trains to football matches, advertised extras such as 'Merrymaker' outings, and mystery excursions respectively. With several large seaside resorts within the area it is no surprise that the East Anglia region is the destination of a considerable number of Adex excursions advertised by various BR regions to bring day trippers to the east coast for a day at the seaside. These have been frequently swelled by mystery excursions, Clacton being a popular destination from such places as far apart as Swansea and Dover. At the beginning of the 1980s these services ran in considerable numbers but the deteriorating monetary climate in more recent times has made the financial gains to be made from running such trains less certain. The numbers of excursion trains have thus dwindled.

Two first division football clubs (at the time of writing) and others in lesser divisions, ensure a steady flow of Footex excursions generated by the clubs to take local supporters to away games and for the transit to matches of supporters from visiting clubs. In an attempt to show the variety of such trains reaching the area Table 1 was compiled depicting the excursions trains arriving in the area during August/September 1981.

The steam museum at Bressingham occasionally attracts arrivals from outside the area to Diss, and excursions have been run in conjunction with Broads cruises, occasional trains running through to Wroxham.

The larger population centres such as Norwich, Colchester and Ipswich have generated appreciable numbers of outgoing Adex trains to enable local people to either visit events, or places of interest, or are run in conjunction with a coach tour within the destination area. A popular excursion in recent years has been an Adex from Ipswich to the Edinburgh Military Tattoo, but again the economic recession with less money available for the public to spend on leisure has meant that the 'Merrymaker' enterprise has had to be reduced. The 1982 programme for the Ipswich area featured just 10 such trains, a substantial reduction when compared to previous years.

Charter Trains/Enthusiasts Specials

As elsewhere on BR, the Norwich Division and other operating authorities with responsibility for East Anglian services, are keen to attract additional revenue by allowing outside bodies to organise special excursions by chartering BR stock for the day. Several local organisations catering for the railway enthusiast make use of this facility either by hiring a main line train for transport to distant destinations or sometimes a DMU for trips within the area. The Wymondham and Dereham Rail Action Committee charter occasional DMU trains to traverse the nominally freight only Dereham branch,

Table 1

Adex/Footex trains to East Anglia, August/September 1981

Date	Type of Train	Destination	Motive Power
30.8.81	Adex	Bicester-Lowestoft (via East Suffolk)	47.096
30.8.81	Adex	Taunton-Yarmouth	47.008
5.9.81	Footex	Barnsley-Norwich	47.219
5.9.81	Footex	Rotherham-Cambridge	47.374
6.9.81	Adex	Oxford-Yarmouth	31.121 and 31.165
16.9.81	Footex	Aberdeen-Ipswich	47.356
26.9.81	Footex	Leeds-Ipswich	37.216

and have hired main line sets for travel to more distant destinations.

Charter specials organised by the railway enthusiast fraternity have brought colour and variety to the East Anglian scene with uncommon motive power for traction or traversing freight only lines.

These tours have brought Class 50s through Bury St Edmunds, 'Deltics' to Norwich, Class 45s on to the GN-GE Joint line, 'Pullman' trains to the Breckland Line and Class 37 locomotive hauled trains on to the freight only Wisbech Branch. Long may such traffic continue!

The Spalding Tulip Parade 1982

Top: On 8 May 1982 Class 40 No 40.052 brought the Keighley & Worth Valley Railway charter from Skipton into Spalding which had arrived via the GN/GE Joint line.
Michael J. Collins

Above: One of the problems of the many specials which arrive at Spalding for the Tulip Parade is the disposal of stock. Many sets have to be stabled at March, Cambridge or Peterborough. This one which arrived from King's Cross behind Class 46 No 46.009 was stabled in the through up siding which once formed the GN line to Boston.
Michael J. Collins

Merrymaker and Football Specials

Above : The 08.00 Ipswich-Shrewsbury footex, running in connection with an FA Cup Tie, passes Kings Dyke, east of Peterborough, with Class 47 No 47.156 complete with appropriate front end decoration on 13 February 1982. *Michael J. Collins*

Above : Waiting for permission to proceed to the station is another Class 46 No 46.051 which arrived at Spalding with a special from New Mills, Manchester *Michael J. Collins*

Below: A Ledbury-Clacton Adex, powered by No 47.111 throughout, runs down the Clacton branch at Hythe on 19 June 1981. *Michael J. Collins*

Right: The 08.05 East Croydon–Great Yarmouth 'Merrymaker' excursion of 12 September 1981 powers through Romford station with Class 47 No 47.158 *Henry Ford* providing traction. On the left a Class 105 twin-car DMU provides the branch service to Upminster. *Michael J. Collins*

Enthusiasts Specials

Above: 'The Joint Line Bumper' special from Plymouth on 13 February 1982 visited the normally freight only Wisbech branch. Photographed negotiating the level crossing outside the closed station at Wisbech, is Class 37 No 37.090 which worked this leg of the excursion. *Michael J. Collins*

Right: Speeding away from the photographic stop at Elsenham is Class 55 'Deltic' No 55.002 *The Kings Own Yorkshire Light Infantry*. In two-tone livery, the locomotive was in charge of the BR sponsored 'Deltic Fenman' from Finsbury Park to Wansford on 2 May 1981.
Michael J. Collins

Left: Class 55 'Deltic' No 55.009 *Alycidon* powers away from Ely towards Queen Adelaide with the 'Deltic Broadsman' special running over two hours late on a freezing December day in 1981. *Chris Burton*

Above: East Anglia saw its first Pullman train for very many years when the SLOA brought its preserved train into the district on 14 August 1982. The train was recorded passing Brandon with No 47.214 in charge, the tour originating in Carlisle and visiting Norwich, Lowestoft and Ipswich.
Michael J. Collins

Left: 14 April 1982 saw the visit of 'The Fenman' enthusiasts' special from York, Wakefield and Leeds hauled by a smartly turned out No 40.081. Although dull, the train was recorded at Chippenham Junction, Newmarket, catching a shaft of sunlight. *Chris Burton*

Behind The Scenes

As elsewhere in the UK, the railway authorities with responsibility for East Anglian lines are charged with the obligation of maintaining the permanent way and other items of fixed equipment to ensure the safe passage of trains. To these ends, a continuous programme of re-ballasting, checking of permanent way, and replacement of defective sections of track has to be adopted to meet the stringent safety requirements on the main lines. If they are to remain passed for high speed running each section of line must be regularly scrutinised and maintained. On main lines such as the GE Norwich line this is carried out every day but secondary lines such as the Harwich Branch are inspected thrice weekly. Much of the work arising from these checks can be dealt with immediately by the Chief Civil Engineer's (CCE) department but more serious work is undertaken away from the public gaze at night during weekends. This is because little traffic runs at this time and therefore traffic dislocation can be kept to a minimum.

Large stocks of spare equipment has to be kept on hand and also expensive items of specialised machinery such as mechanical diggers, ballast cleaners, ballast tamping machines and cranes have to be available. Therefore the CCE department has a number of depots within the region at strategic points for the storage and upkeep of such materials. One of the largest depots is situated at Chesterton Junction, Cambridge, while subsidiary sites at Ipswich and Norwich are also used. For use in the

Permanent Way and Equipment Maintenance

Below: A permanent way train including a ballast cleaner proceeds 'wrong line' on the GE main line at Manningtree with Class 31 No 31.269 at the head on 6 August 1980. Note the LNER type wooden coach complete with Gresley bogies coupled within the formation. *Michael J. Collins*

south of the region, much of the necessary equipment is stored at Leyton CCE depot, East London, while the specialised equipment for keeping overhead wiring and catenary in good order is stored alongside the main line at Romford.

As in other industries maintenance work has to be carried out 'within budget' and financial constraints in the 1980s have meant that work required away from the more heavily used main lines has been postponed for lack of investment capital. Therefore fixed equipment on many of the lesser lines within East Anglia is now in poor shape. The result of this has been that the authorities have been forced to impose severe speed restrictions at some locations both to maintain safety standards and minimise further wear and tear. In spite of the 'patch and make do' philosophy that has been forced on the railway in the face of severe fiscal policies, the main lines in East Anglia are still receiving adequate maintenance work. Sections of the very busy GE main line south of Colchester have been recently passed for 100mph running but in contrast non-essential track work, on parts of the line with less traffic, have been postponed where safety considerations permit.

In addition to routine maintenance BR have embarked on more ambitious projects during the 1980s. The new Cambridge power box, completed during October 1982, will ultimately control signalling from just south of Ely to Bishop's Stortford covering in addition lines to Royston and Fulbourne. When the whole scheme is completed fourteen manual signalboxes will be replaced and six level crossings will be supervised by closed circuit television from Cambridge. A further resignalling scheme is in hand at the time of writing based on a £15 million scheme at Colchester. Work commenced in Spring 1981 and the two-storey brick built power box constructed as part of the project will initially replace 11 manually operated boxes. It will cover a total of 35 route miles from Colchester, through Ipswich to Claydon and also the branch from Manningtree to Harwich. Future extensions will allow the new box to ultimately control 95 route miles from Chelmsford to Diss with adjoining branch lines.

Despite the financial rigours of the 1980s the BR Research and Technical Centre at Derby has continued to investigate methods of cutting costs or improving services provided for the travelling public. The labour intensive branches of East Anglia have become subject to particular attention in both fields. The East Suffolk line has been used in a number of experiments because it makes an ideal case study due to its sparse traffic and the lengthy distance available for investigation. The many level crossings on the line has led to an experiment to evaluate the use of radio signals to operate crossing gates by an approaching train. Concern about the condition of BR's ageing fleet of DMUs led to the same line being

Below: A splendid photograph of Class 40 No 40.096 on the Ely-Cambridge line with an up ballast train consisting mainly of 'mermaid' wagons on 16 March 1982. *Kim Fullbrook*

used again from 13 October to 12 December 1980 when it was utilised to test passenger reaction to the BR experimental railbus (alias Lightweight Experimental Vehicle LEV-1). It was thought that this vehicle may well be a way of replacing DMUs with minimum cost because the vehicle utilised a substantial number of road bus components. During these months the bus was used for the first time ever on an advertised passenger service although it subsequently ran in other parts of the country after modifications had been completed. While in East Anglia the bus made a daily weekday return run from Ipswich to Lowestoft and worked an evening turn to Saxmundham and back.

Above: Class 37 No 37.110 powers a westbound rail train along the Cambridge-Chippenham Junction line at Fulbourne on 4 June 1982. *Kim Fullbrook*

Left: Every year the permanent way has to be sprayed with weed killer to discourage the formation of damaging plant growth on the track bed. The weedkilling train is being propelled through Reedham, Norfolk, on 13 May 1982 by an unidentified Class 37 locomotive. *Geoff Pinder*

Above left: Sometimes the overhead wires need attention and on 13 June 1982 an up EMU brought down the wires at New Hall Loop, Chelmsford. This meant the attendance of the Romford CCE Dept electrification train, with Class 31 No 31.148 in charge, which can be seen in the background. *Michael J. Collins*

Above: Severe winter weather brings its own problems and in this photograph Class 37 No 37.050 coupled inside the Colchester snow ploughs returns back to base on 10 January 1982 after clearing drifts on the Sudbury Branch. *Michael J. Collins*

Left: During an icy blast on 9 December 1981 this fine signal gantry at Coldham Lane, Cambridge, froze solid and needed attention by the S&T Department. Class 37 No 37.023 and Class 08 No 08.240 stabled at the adjacent depot look on. *Barry J. Nicolle*

Above: Occasionally engineering work outside the East Anglia region has its effect in the form of extra traffic being diverted away from the trouble. A Class 254 HST unit forming the Sunday 08.15 Newcastle-King's Cross approaches Ely on such an occasion on 27 September 1981. *John C. Baker*

Miscellanea

Below: Class 31 No 31.318 eases through Cambridge station with a special train conveying brand new Class 315 EMUs Nos 315.840 and 315.841 from York Yard North to Stratford Old Yard on 25 September 1981. *Barry J. Nicolle*

Left: A former Class 100 two-car set formed from carriages Nos 51122/56300 was, after withdrawal, taken into departmental service and renumbered 975664 and 975637 and dubbed 'The Stourton Saloon'. The unit was photographed passing Newport (Essex), as the General Manager's Saloon on 28 July 1981. *Colin J. Marsden*

Below: Class 47 No 47.278 arrives at Thorpe-le-Soken with the 'Mentor' (Mobile Electronic Network Tester and Observation Recorder) train after traversing the Walton-on-Naze branch on 20 July 1980. *John D. Mann*

Above: British Leyland and BR built a single-car four-wheeled 'Railbus' from two standard Leyland National bus bodies, mounted on a specially adapted four-wheel wagon underframe. Test running on passenger service took place on the East Suffolk line to assess passenger reaction. One such working was photographed at Westerfield on 24 September 1980. *Michael J. Collins*

Below: A development of the railbus was the two-car Class 140 DMU prototype, again built from Leyland National bus body components. The unit was recorded passing Brinkley Crossing, near Six Mile Bottom, on a demonstration run from Chippenham Junction to Cambridge on 8 July 1981. *John C. Baker*